CW01022517

If the Corncrake Calls

If the Corncrake Calls

Ian Niall

Compiled and edited by Sheila Pehrson

Foreword by Douglas Dunn

First published in 2016 by

an imprint of
Neil Wilson Publishing Ltd
www.nwp.co.uk

© The Estate of Ian Niall 2016
Foreword © Douglas Dunn 2016
Introduction © Sheila Pehrson 2016

All illustrations © the estate of Barbara Greg 2016
Cover illlustration © Hazel Campbell 2016

The authors have established their moral right to be
identified as the authors of this work.

ISBN: 978-1-906000-94-3
Ebook ISBN: 978-1-906000-95-0

Printed and bound in the EU

CONTENTS

Here are descriptions of natural life: in woodlands
and fields, and in the landscapes of mountains and
water. From the hare in its form to the pigeons
'carried across the undulating country by the
buffeting wind' and the trout rising in the black
water of a mountain lake, Ian Niall is never more in
his element.

Some of these men were his childhood heroes, some
were kindred spirits and all we can recognise. We
may have seen them loitering, just as Snib or Black
Bill did, with an eye to the almost invisible main
chance. On the edge of society, they are, in their way,
universal characters to be found in any country
village or along a road in any remote rural
backwater. They are celebrated here with a knowing
understanding and a gentle humour.

These memoir pieces describe the writer's growth from child to adult. They show us a solitary child, his growing attachment to the natural world, and the seasonal routine and daily rituals of a farming life more in keeping with the 19th century than the 20th.

Whether it is observation of the rising hay 'dotted with yellow-flowered weeds and seeding thistles', the 'contour of the ground with its ridges of a past season's ploughing', the 'loose stones about your heels' or a description of the awe-inspiring emptiness of a remote landscape, the importance of place in Ian Niall's writing cannot be ignored.

The first chapter of Ian Niall's first novel. It was published under his own name, John McNeillie, when he was 22 years old. Amongst other things it shows us how he drew upon his time at North Clutag to tell his story.

Foreword

FROM THE FIRST PARAGRAPH of his first book —
Wigtown Ploughman: Part of His Life (1939) — it's clear that
John McNeillie was an astute observer of nature. Happily,
the first chapter of that powerful novel is included in this
selection of his writing edited with expertise and affection
by his daughter. It was a controversial book in its time,
depicting episodes of psychotic behaviour caused by pover-
ty, poor housing, hardship, and exaggerated masculinity. It
was also drawn from childhood and youthful experience of
rural life in the Machars of Wigtownshire, that triangular
protuberance dangling between Luce Bay and Wigtown Bay.

McNeillie's adoption of his pen name Ian Niall, in the
late 1940s, appears to have coincided with a rejection of
'realism' in favour of a more 'poetic' prose, a change in his
priorities. It is to be doubted if that is the whole story.
Nature, in Tennyson's phrase, can be 'red in tooth and claw',
even on these temperate islands; and Niall never flinches
from that natural fact. Of an owl, he writes:

> You come upon his roost to see him leaving. If he is
> forced into the open in daylight half the small birds go
> with him to make his life a hell. They are right to mob
> him, for he is a great killer, an enemy of the wood as
> much as the hawk, more powerful, more ruthless than
> the rusty barn owl. This stump of a bleary-eyed owl can
> slaughter the blackbird. He has eaten many a squirrel

and has no fear of man when he thrusts his hand into his tree trunk nest.

Much of Niall's intimacy with nature derived from poaching. Whether with snare, gun, rod and line, guddling or tickling for trout, or rabbiting with ferrets for the pot, or for the thrill of it, poaching is a nocturnal activity or an experience of the early hours. It puts its practitioners in a position of dangerous solitude. For a short time the poacher knows the discomforts of a time before 'civilisation'; he becomes easy with the perils and excitements of the primitive hunter. Gamekeepers know this too; but they are on opposing sides, although there is a large middle ground, a shared knowledge of land, its lore, and its creatures.

An extreme familiarity with natural life and terrain is what made Ian Niall an authentic prose poet of the wild and unowned. Writing of a hare, he says: 'All this is his country. He shares it with others, but it is his, fallow and arable, fir plantings and whin waste. It is his, as it belongs to everyone who crosses it on a sunlit morning.'

Niall's son, Andrew McNeillie, in his biography of his father, estimates that Niall published at least two million words of journalism in his lifetime. Ironically, much of it appeared in the form of 'Notes' contributed to *Country Life*, that is, to a readership of the county set – landowners – and suburbanite fantasists dreaming of country piles and landed estates enticingly illustrated in advertisements of properties for sale.

At a time when nature writing is necessarily in vogue, Sheila Pehrson's selection from her father's writing offers a wonderful opportunity to read a modern master of the genre.

Douglas Dunn

Introduction

TAKE A FEW LINES FROM the extended essays of the writer Ian Niall and you might be reading the lines of a song or a poem:

> They are all wild, the hare of the rough wet hollows, the hare of the clover hill and the hare of the cold mountain, wild like the cry of the peewit and the sad and lonely flight of the heron.

> The grass tops sway a little in the earth-close breeze and are still again. Summer has gone and no grasshopper sings.

> The owl makes no more sound than the moth.

The images are drawn delicately. They are haunting and elegiac. They evoke the steady eye of a naturalist. Put these lines back into their context and they reveal the craftsmanship of a writer of exceptional prose.

If the Corncrake Calls is an anthology of pieces largely taken from Ian Niall's non-fiction books. They describe the natural world, people and places, and an early childhood spent on a remote farmstead in Wigtownshire, Scotland, in the early 1920s. They also reveal both the time and landscape that shaped the writer he became. The extracts are arranged by theme, and throughout I have tried to ensure that they connect well and that wherever possible there is a link, however slight, between them. I have included just one piece of his fiction to add to this, the first chapter from his first novel.

Ian Niall's real name was John McNeillie. He was born in 1916 and his early childhood was spent at North Clutag, the farm tenanted by his grandfather in Wigtownshire. His removal there was in his best interests. A younger sister had meningitis, and his mother, my grandmother, was expecting a third child. My father was around three years old when he left his family in Old Kilpatrick, near Dalmuir, to live on the farm. This was the place that he would come to regard as home. He was eight years old when he returned to his parents and thereafter made the journey back to North Clutag in the school holidays. Here he enjoyed the freedom of the open fields, moors and woodlands. He befriended the men that worked for his grandfather, the ploughmen, the byremen and the itinerant workers, and enjoyed the companionship of family, friends and visitors. John McNeillie, now separate from his siblings, was a solitary child. This period of his life he came to regard as an idyllic time, an intensely experienced and happy rural childhood. In later years these experiences would come to dominate his non-fiction and earn him a place in the tradition of ruralist writing. In the late 1930s, he married and moved to live in North Wales where he also found inspiration in the Welsh countryside and amongst the Welsh country people.

John McNeillie became a journalist on the *West Middlesex Gazette* when he left school at the age of 17. His ambition was to write books and he did. When he was 22 years old Putnam of London and New York published the first of his three early novels, under his own name. It was called *Wigtown Ploughman: Part of his Life* and it caused a small sensation . . .

Set in the Machars of Wigtownshire, Scotland and particularly in the locality of Malzie school, the Malzie farms and the district bounded by Wigtown, Kirkcowan, Mochrum, Port William and Sorbie, this is the story of part of a life of a ploughman, son of a cotman. Cotfolk are the dwellers in the small stone cottages which house the agricultural workers of the north. Part of the life of a simple man of the soil, this story refers to no particular ploughman, for all are not great fighters, poachers, drunkards or wife beaters. This story is an attempt to portray something of the best and the worst in them.

Here real and imagined worlds intertwine and the young novelist's attempt to portray something of the 'best and the worst' struck a raw nerve with his readers in Scotland, and indeed with the wider world. The story is interspersed with pastoral interludes describing work at the plough, collecting whaup eggs and visits to the shore, but it also describes poor housing, desperate living conditions, immorality and violence among the cotfolk and agricultural workers. (More about this can be found in the 'Introduction, Notes and Appendices' by Andrew McNeillie in the paperback edition of *Wigtown Ploughman*, published by Birlinn in 2012). For our purposes here, suffice it to say that his critics were divided. The subsequent uproar, while it provoked improvements in social conditions, must have overshadowed the good press he received for a promising first novel.

By the 1950s he was enjoying recognition and critical approval. He changed his publisher to Heinemann, and his writing name to Ian Niall, and began what would become a more than 40-year run of weekly articles for *Country Life* magazine. His novel *No Resting Place* published by Heinemann in 1948, a story of travelling people in rural

Wigtownshire, was made into a film in Ireland by Paul Rotha that went on to represent Britain at the Venice Film Festival. And in this decade he also completed his three volumes of extended essay-form books, *The Poacher's Handbook*, *Fresh Woods* and *Pastures New*.

Ian Niall would go on to write about the natural world and to write memoir and more novels. He would write about fly-fishing in the Welsh mountain lakes, wild fowling and country pursuits, and would continue to call upon his years spent at North Clutag, although he never would again provide his readers with so detailed a road map. In 1998 he was awarded an honorary doctorate of letters from Glasgow University for his contribution to Scottish literature.

★ ★ ★

There is a sense in which Niall's nature writing is proprietorial. David Profumo comments in his review of *Fresh Woods* and *Pastures New*, published together by Little Toller Books in 2012.

> He evokes 'the pattern of survival' with his fine web of words. Of an old rusty-backed hare, he writes: 'All this is his country. He shares it with others, but it is his, fallow and arable, fir plantings and whin waste, mossy knowes and king-cup hollows. It is his, as it belongs to everyone who crosses it on a sunlit morning.'

Profumo goes on to say, 'He might have been describing himself.' It is tempting to go a little further and to suggest that this 'pattern of survival' is also, in part, his. That John McNeillie, as he fixed his young eye on the natural world, discovered a world more secure and permanent than his own. He recalls being three years old when 'the Big Hill was in corn' but in writing of this time he gives no space to the trauma he undoubtedly experienced when he was separated from his mother, or to the confusion he must have felt as he adapted to a new way of life with people he hardly knew. Only once does he mention 'yelling for my mother'. Instead he describes what might be called a transference of his affections.

> The Wee Field was my playground. It had everything a child could desire, round hillocks of gorse, gentle slopes, a drystone wall, a thorn hedge, a burn with peaty banks, places where laying-away hens nested, waterholes where the ducks left their eggs. Here the wagtail pinned his nest above the burn and here were the holes of the water vole.

This was no ordinary playground. Here he set his first snare under the watchful eye of his grandmother and chased 'wild bees with a wide-necked bottle filled with clover heads and sugar'. An extra seat was fitted to the binder 'so that I could sit beside my grandfather and go to and fro across the Big Hill as the corn was cut'.

There is never a sense that Ian Niall learnt about nature in order to write about it, or that his literary ambition was to put the place of his childhood in the public eye. What does come through in his non-fiction is his deep impulse to tell the story of the world that was his, that was integral to him, and the words to do this spilled out of him. For all the lyricism of this writing a small part of the realism that haunted his first novel is never far away.

No matter how beautiful, no matter how fragrant the breath of the whin field, we were practical people. A day came when the gorse had to be halted. The outlying clumps were attacked by a whin hoe. The hills themselves were set on fire.

The piece of moss my grandfather rented was in a hollow. It was used for years and the peat was in terraces. In very wet weather the lower parts flooded. No one knew how deep the moss was. The primeval forests that had made it must have lasted an age, for in dry weather it was impossible to cut below the peat. Now and then the cutters might find what we called a moss-block and effort was always made to dig it out for winter fires. These blocks were really ancient trees, perhaps oak that had sunk into the decaying forest and become almost petrified. As hard as stone they were. After a saw had been used on a moss-block it was useless for anything else and my grandfather always swore that there was a second heat in them, the first being the heat engendered trying to cut them into a suitable size for burning.

Robert Macfarlane, in his review of John McNeillie's *My Childhood* (published posthumously in 2004) from which the last quotation is taken, recalls that Seamus Heaney was an admirer of this book and described 'North Clutag' as an 'alternative Mossbawn'. Macfarlane comments upon the 'affinity between these two poetic parochial parishes' and goes on to say how both men shared 'the same belief in the significance of touch and labour – "heft" and "graft" – as ways of experiencing the world'.

Niall's close observations of the natural world reveal his understanding of the interconnectivity of wild life, and of man's place in this too. He writes well about the passing of a world and the passing of a time, and now and again flags up his concern about the impact of 'progress' upon the peace and wellbeing of the countryside he so loved. In 1987 he wrote: 'Suitable habitat is vital to all creatures. Alas, we rarely concern ourselves with the fact that our own habitat may be threatened by our shortsightedness'.

Elsewhere he bemoans the loss of the remote, the 'sound of silence' gone to the 'thunderous arrival of black, sinister fighter bombers that skim down the valleys', 'terrifying sheep' and 'banishing ravens'. It is perhaps little wonder that his writing chimes with us now.

By way of a postscript to all of the above I leave you with this quotation from *The Way of a Countryman* and wish you a good read:

We lived in a part of the country to which the latest inventions permeated slowly. Farming methods were old-fashioned by standards elsewhere. There were still as many tilting reapers in the corn as there were binders and although most farmers had reapers it was not unknown for two or three mowers to be given a five-acre field of ryegrass to cut. Bog hay was always scythed. The 'crakes had a time to incubate and lead their young away while the mowers swung and lurched their way into the long grass. Even the hay reaper would bog down and choke its knives in some fields. The corncrakes stalked through the forest of fine grass without great alarm. They brought off their broods and led them to safety and they came again, summer after summer, until the reaping machines were improved and men who could mow with scythes went to their long rest.

Sheila Pehrson
Lower Shiplake
August 2016

There is a little hill in the low planting, a hill that is itself a forest of bracken as tall as a man: bend low and you see the world of the rabbit, the stoat, the pheasant.
Fresh Woods

Down in the heart of the little planting the pheasant materialises. There is no other word for his reappearance. One minute the brown slope running to the blackberry is bare and the next the pheasant is there, softly, gently, the slightest movement of a stalk of grass. He walks a stately pace or two, his tail sweeping the ground, halts, listens. The bright eye moves, the blood-red comb and head feathers rise and the tail lifts as he goes. What shades of blue, and chestnut brown, and that neck ring, like the brand on the wood pigeon, the mark on the grass snake. The sounds of the wood are sounds he knows, the stone rocking as a rabbit bobs over into the moss, the scolding of the squirrels, the sharp scorn of the jay.
Fresh Woods

1
The World of the Rabbit, the Stoat, the Pheasant
… and the Ways of Fish and Fishermen

THE HARE RUNS THE GRASS HILL and sleeps in a fold of ground in a bed as snug, as sheltered, as that of the little field mouse. Here a clump of hay-brown grass stands alone and conspicuous, but you can see through it. You can see the contour of the grounds with its ridges of a past season's ploughing where the vetch and yarrow grow. The grass tops sway a little in the earth-close breeze and are still again. Summer has gone and no grasshopper sings. Right in the middle of the clump of grass lies the hare. His haunches are raised and his ears smooth on his neck. He is soft brown, darker brown, matched to the grass, its seeds more silvery at the tips; matched to the ground, every beautiful hair a blend with the surroundings. He sleeps in the warmth of the October or late September noon.

The scents of the field soothe him, and the senses of the hunter are drugged by the breath of the land, the scents of decay, of dying leaves and mushroom growth, by the very beauty of the shades of feeble autumn, the little red fungus on the fragment of twig, the stubble bleaching fawn. This one is the hare of the arable fields. The one from the bogs seems taller of leg and darker. When he rears among the rushes, pausing on the patch of hair grass to take a message from the wind, he seems a bigger animal. As he moves in through the rushes he retains that impression of stature. The hare of the mountain is certainly smaller. He is grey and has a tinge of blue. He reminds those who see him of blots of frozen snow up where the air is cold and the streams are sheathed in a covering of ice. They are all wild, the hare of the rough wet hollows, the hare of the clover hill and the hare of the cold mountain, wild like the cry of the peewit and the sad and lonely flight of the heron.

One will have his sleeping place on the southern slope of a distant hill, and another in the wood where the bracken has folded upon itself in a clearing. Their movement out of wood or across the brow will be a thing so graceful that when you see it for the first time you will stand and stare long after they are gone. You will not often get close enough to see the hare in his form. He will be gone while you clamber the dry-stone wall and bring loose stones about your heels. His long back legs will take him fast across the hollow, the shadow of a wind-driven cloud, through the gap and away, running easily for the meadow and the shelter of the longer grass. When you have steadied your heartbeat and brushed the grey moss of the stones from your flanks you will walk past the spot where he sleeps from mid-morn until afternoon. It will be warm with the heat of his fur and if you come and disturb it with your fumbling hands it is likely that tomorrow he will sleep elsewhere at noon, so it is well, perhaps, that you are blind to such things.

The Poacher's Handbook

Down there in the bog a finch is searching for seeds on a bed of early-maturing weed, a hare is loping in the sunlight, going leisurely away in the safety of the ear-high forest about him, crossing the little clearings, leaving his print on the soft black earth.

Pastures New

Watch the hare in the middle morning when the sun is up and he begins to think of going to his form. We cannot tell how far he has gone by night, but now, when the sun is on the southern slope, oblique and yellow, touching the feathery grass, we can watch him coming back, for he is the hare from the high wood and he slips away in the bracken as silently as a partridge vanishing down a potato drill or a waterhen going into the rushes. We go with the hare to see him enter the wood, to see him settle and sleep. He belongs to the high wood, this tall, rusty-backed hare. He belongs as the kestrel belongs, making his home here for a season, escaping the snare, the yelping of dogs set after him on a Sunday afternoon, the poacher's gun. He is not young. Beneath his skin he carries a few pills of four or five shot. One of his soft brown ears is scarred with a shot wound. His family runs the hills and plains as the high bird's call sounds, and he knows every long furrow, every drain hollow, every dike hole and hedge gap, from here to the horizon. No stream roars in spate but he knows a place to cross; no ditch divides a moss but he can clear it at a bound as he races before the lurcher dog. All this is his country. He shares it with others, but it is his, fallow and arable, fir plantings and whin waste, mossy knowes and kingcup hollows. It is his, as it belongs to everyone who crosses it on a sunlit morning.
Fresh Woods

Put your cap on your head and call the dog. It is cold across the fields, put a scarf round your neck and make sure that your boots are comfortable. We are ready, with our snack in our pocket and all of a bright day before us. The little field behind the house wets our feet with its dewy grass, a startled rabbit goes bouncing off to the warren above the ditch. The sounds are the sounds of spring and the morning is as light-hearted as the bird singing on the tip of the tall gorse. On the hill the peewits are calling, half of them in the air and half along the furrows. Study the beauty of this bird, the contrast of black and white, the jauntiness of his tuft and the madness of his flights. His note is spring itself. The peewit nests not only on the ploughed land and the pasture. He nests in the rough and on the moss. If we fail to find him in the arable field we have only to climb the march wall and go on into the moss.

Pastures New

Half-way up the first hill we see a pair of birds running the furrow. The cock bird rises and sweeps in over our heads. His call is urgent. The black and white of his feathers is all we see, for our eyes are quickly on the ground. We cross the furrow and come back. The air is filled with the cries of a dozen pairs of birds. In this field we might find one. The peewit has a habit of making false nests or depressions in the earth. Country lads call them 'cock' nests, but from the false nests or the real one neither bird ever rises. They run and rise twenty yards away. While we are walking to the field the birds are moving. When we are on the ploughing they are rising with cries designed to attract us as far from the eggs as possible. The first nest is right before you. One more step and your foot would have crushed the eggs. Look at them. Are they not wonderful? Four eggs as near a blend with the ground as could be. They are pointed and, like the egg of the curlew, larger for the size of the bird that laid them. Turn these eggs so that their points are outwards, leave the place and return, and you will see that the hen has carefully turned them point-inwards again. They are made this way so that they will not roll away. The hen sits comfortably on them until they hatch and as soon as the chicks are out they can look after themselves; at least, they can run and crouch on the earth and blend with the ground about them so well that until they move they are invisible.

Pastures New

The kestrel sails above the trees and a sparrow hawk comes down the hollow, making a score of small birds fly ahead in a cloud of terror.

Fresh Woods

The forest of the oatfield probably protects more helpless creatures in summer than all the other fields of the country-side. The time between sowing and harvest brings so many things to life in a state of comparative helplessness that, were it not for the cover of the growing crop, the preying animals and birds would slaughter them by the thousand. The owl hunts the open pasture, but scores of mice evade him, down in the security of the stalks of the oats. He could plunge down after them, but the heads of the corn would fold under his wings and protect the scampering mouse. He wastes no time over the corn. The kestrel, too, knows that it is useless to hover there and the stoat and the weasel do not venture to hunt because there the scents are confusing, the sounds are muffled by the gentle rubbing of a million stalks and the whispering of ten million ears of corn. The mouse thrives, the beetle goes unmolested, the larva develops, the fly hatches and harvest bug and harvest mouse live to believe that summer is for ever, an eternal breeze swaying the yellowing corn, the voice of the corncrake unending.

Pastures New

If the corncrake calls, summer is young and the oats half grown. To go in search of him is to chase the rainbow, seek the water shrew or find the cuckoo's egg. The corncrake belongs to the elusive world of animals and birds. It is hard to see and identify the water shrew, for he floats across the pool like a brown shadow, a dead leaf pulled by an invisible thread. The crake calls and the man in the hollow looks up and listens. It is a sound that the busy world does not know. Fewer and fewer are the numbers of those who have heard it and hear it yet. Indeed, I have not heard the corncrake myself for many summers. It is eight or nine years since I saw him here in Wales.

In those days there were fewer tractors. The hill farms were quiet. Horses still pulled the roller and the reaper. I walked uphill along the side of a wood. The corn was half ripe and yet not tall, for it was growing on poor ground. The crake rose at my feet, flew ahead and settled on a bare patch. I watched him. He darted forward through some thistles and went on among stunted gorse to the hedge bottom. I stood long after he was gone, fixing every detail in my mind. I am not a bird watcher in the strict sense. I knew that this experience might not come again because the bird was rare already. I did not hear the call in the locality either before I saw the crake or after, and I have wondered since whether the corncrake can breed in a place and not be heard. Perhaps not. The thought is a pleasant one, a fancy that makes the extermination of the land rail kind less definite.

When the fields of home were one third under the plough every year, and two thirds of the ploughing seeded in corn, the crake was often there. The call is old. Somehow it suggests to me a scene of agriculture as it was when the harvest came down to the scythe and was threshed with a flail on a winnowing floor. I think of it now and remember the summer evening with the air almost still, the peat smoke going up from the kitchen chimney, the midges beneath the branches of the apple trees in the garden down the road, and the footpath below the stile perfumed with the scent of honeysuckle that twined so thickly in the thorn hedge that the trees were strangled.

The first time I ever heard it I was told that it was the corncrake. No one thought anything of the fact. The crakes came every year. They were out there in the old road field, in the Barness Field, the Big Hill, the Switchback Hill. The call was hardly more remarkable than the call of the partridge. The partridge call meant that a covey was being reared in one of the nearby fields. The corncrake would not make a supper when September came. The sound had no special significance any more than had the purring of the nightjar.

Pastures New

We came to see the birds, we came to loiter among the trees and see the last streaks of day.

Fresh Woods

The owl makes no more sound than the moth. He launches himself like a ghost from his perch, turns a wing to clear a branch and goes down the woodside. Unless you happen to look in that particular direction he goes unseen. His going and coming are unearthly. You turn and find him veering out over the field, brown and a blend with the night, soundless and so hard to see that it seems the night has opened and swallowed him. Sometimes he calls, but he is more of a silent creature than the wood owl, as he is called. He sits like an old man resting, top-heavy, about to topple from his perch, dozing and unwary, but he is not. He has all the light he wants in those almost shut eyes, at least by day. He hears as well as any bird. You come upon his roost to see him leaving. If he is forced into the open in daylight half the small birds go with him to make his life a hell. They are right to mob him, for he is a great killer, an enemy of the wood as much as the hawk, more powerful, more ruthless than the rusty barn owl. This tree-stump of a bleary-eyed owl can slaughter the blackbird. He has eaten many a squirrel and has no fear of man when he thrusts a hand into his tree trunk nest.

Fresh Woods

The wood comes to life, but the grass snake calls it a day. Perhaps she has enjoyed her last bit of summer warmth, for lethargy is infecting her. The first little whisper of a cooler breeze, the hand of winter, so hard to detect, is putting just a degree of coldness in the earth. The sun's heat has gone a fraction earlier that it did yesterday and the leaf has changed a shade from dark green to lighter green a thing so slight that it seems that the leaf is not dying but that the light on its surface is getting brighter, here in the depths.

Fresh Woods

Over the brow of the hill. Do you hear the bird singing in the high wood? Down below it is dark, night among the elderberry bushes and the blackthorns. Summer night in the high wood, warm and alive. In the little patch of sky the leaves of the beech look black and flutter gently. Out on the turnip field it is impossible to see the rabbit or the hare but the leaves rustle and tremble, the yellow weeds sway. The night is full of the little sounds that mark the season, the fly-ing beetle's note as it goes off speeding through the gloom, the cry of lambs on the grass hills, a restless dog barking in the hollow drum of a barn or a cart-shed, the far-away and yet weirdly near sound of two countrymen talking at a road end. The bird sings and some oddness in the air makes its heart happy. The last combing of the day goes from the sky and the bird is silent. The owl calls. The wood sits brooding, shelter-ing its bird life, its millions of insects. The tawny owl flies, the wild cat hunts. Who has time in his life to discover how far the rabbit ranges at night, the territory covered by the hare? Who can tell what world the owl sees as he perches on the stump like a ghost, or why he does so when he is so lately out of roost, for night for him is day and day night? Does it become a brighter place of monochrome, like moonlight, and does he sit contemplating its beauty and peacefulness? One half of the world goes to sleep and the other half awakes. Here in the crumbling bank the wasps' nest settles. It is not completely dormant. It is still alive, vibrating, humming gen-tly. Part of the pattern of night and day, scavengers of sticky jam pot shards and midden refuse, food for the badger, dis-traction for the honey bee, grubs for the hungry fish, a hot noon fury to warn the browsing beast away.

Fresh Woods

It grows colder. The leaves are flying from the thorn tree and the stubble is getting old. There is no life in the high wood and the stoat will soon be in his white. We can go to the wood at the tail of the loch to see the duck and the big bog hare. Look across the country and see the neat cornstacks in the stackyards, the hard appearance of the river, and the way the hedges have become thin. There is a shiver on the land after noon, and the brightness of the west is brief. The geese are due out of the north and the old man, his blood thin, remembers the winter he saw the snow bunting in his garden, pink and beautiful, but so numerous that the superstitious shook their heads.

Fresh Woods

To the people of the far north it is winter when the geese pass. There is something ominous in the sound that heralds their coming. The tundra is being reclaimed by the cold hand of winter, the northern seas are boiling, putting salt into the gale, and the lashing rain that sweeps in soon carries sleet. In a matter of days desolation returns to the bogs and the plains where once midges thronged. Hills and mountains, rocks and crags are glazed with snow like some vast piece of confectionery, and the geese have gone south just as the petrels move before the storm. The breeding grounds are on the brink of the endless night and only very special forms of life are equipped to survive there. As the migrants come south every goose on the farm pasture hears their crying and stops grazing the turf to call in reply. This, too, is one of the sad sounds of dying autumn. The fat Emden and the Toulouse would take to the air if they could, but, alas, they are no more equipped to join the flight than a portly stockbroker is equipped to hunt the mountain for his food.

The pathos in the exchanges is something never to be forgotten and it persists while the migrants are approaching, as they pass overhead and go on out of sight. In the last minutes the talk of geese is a poignant, tragic conversation. It may take a little time, but the endless waves end, and somehow to me it always seemed that when this happened the sky took on a darker colouring, the sun lost its brilliance as the domestic geese fell silent again. Anyone who sees the passing geese is stirred not simply by the trailing lines of birds crossing the heavens, taking their bearings and slowly altering their flight line, but by primitive and primeval instincts. No doubt something other than the calendar and the falling of the leaves or the breaking of the bud gives a similar stimulus to the peasant of France or Italy who looks on the vineyard or the olive grove and knows, perhaps by the sound of a seasonable wind or the behaviour of a bird, that the eternal cycle of change is taking place.

The Way of a Countryman

In the last days of winter or the first of spring the partridges pair. Winter and spring have a demarcation on a calendar but in the year they are a breath of warmth across a hill, the snowdrops wild on the fringe of a wood, a primrose opening and the partridges rising from the fawn of an old stubble hill and sailing down over a hedge to a new territory. Spring is in the hedge and the mellowing day just as the last of winter is in the solitary woodcock springing from the beech leaves and going off in his heavy twisting flight through the spaces between trees and bushes. In these early days of the year the first partridge pair would come to the Wee Five Acre, along the hollow, fast, wind-borne, swinging up to clear the drystone wall, gliding into its shelter and going on, as beautiful as anything that flies, to the tall broom, the lean thorn on the Wee Five Acre's edge.

Pastures New

Once at the ditch the waterhen knows how to vanish. She is down in the water in an instant, along the bank and into the roots of the overhanging tree. She follows the water, through the crowding blackberry, under the beard of the whins, away in the secret places where the grass does not grow and the black peat bank is mined by the vole and here and there a rabbit hole comes out right above the water.

Pastures New

Perhaps the most secretive of all birds is the water rail. He is commoner than the countryman thinks, but he steers his way in through the rushes and reeds and is gone, like a cunning old poacher or the fox in the thick bracken. The first time I ever saw the water rail was in the bog. It was a dead bird, stretched across a little patch of yellow round rush. I picked up the carcass and examined it. The water rail has something of the waterhen about its build. It is a finer thing and its whole appearance goes with its secretive habits. Its body seems unbalanced, for its thighs are short and its legs long in the lower joint. Its beak is red or orange in hue. The brown of its back is not unlike the brown of the hen pheasant and on its sides it has grey and white feathers that give the impression of horizontal, alternate bars of these colours. Its front is grey, the grey of a mouse. On the tail is a mark of white, although the contrast is much greater in the waterhen than in the rail. On the ground the rail runs quickly. Its flight is low, a sort of scurrying away through the weeds or along the course of the water. It does not go far. Like the jack snipe its flight is short, but try and find the water rail once it has entered a marsh! The toad that jerks his way into a pool submerges and blends with the weed and mud about him, but the chicks of the waterhen have it, the young of the plover. The master of camouflage and concealment does his work as only a master can. The helpless things of the world are well protected.

Pastures New

Next to the way they spring almost vertically into the air the most impressive thing about the little teal, the smallest duck, is the furious rush of their arrival.

A Fowler's World

From their nature fowl are great frequenters of estuaries – broad expanses of sand cut by the river hurrying after the tide, by the very maw of the sea that draws into it the water from a thousand hills and upland pastures. Away out beyond the last bush or tree, the last rock rolled in the icecap, long banks of shingle graduate to tail-ends of gravel and the water, brackish a mile back, is as salt as the sea. Away out here, swimming merrily against the current in the shallows, a duck or two will feed. Farther out a raft of duck may lie at roost like moored craft, all dozing with their necks relaxed, bills on their breasts or turned back across a wing. The estuary is like the very rim-edge of the world, safe from surprise with miles and miles of skyline across which every-thing comes and goes, the solitary steamer trailing smoke, or a lonely seabird on its private journey from one out-of-sight headland to the next. The tide murmurs and flows to quicksand. The light is bright, and the land far away.

A Fowler's World

Study the mallard as she goes to and fro from her nest and watch how she leads the young away the moment they are water-borne, for she wastes no time doing this. Almost as soon as the last shell has dried out the brood has vanished. This is because a waterbird has many enemies. A fox will search the marsh for a duck's nest. The carrion crow patrolling overhead may miss the eggs hidden in the covering of down, but the crow and the black-backed gull, to say nothing of the stoat, the rat, the heron and other ravenous creatures, will search for the dappled ducklings from the moment they hatch until they can fend for themselves on open water. The mallard has been conditioned to persecution since the first swamp island showed above water and it has survived because it has discovered how to survive. It is wary, watchful, keen-sighted, a master of the art of taking cover and getting away without making a disturbance. This is the fowl you must study if you are to be a fowler, the elusive bird of the reeds and rushes, the bird of the night and half light, the bird that sometimes walks abroad on the inundated pasture and takes wing from the ditch when you least expect it. When it comes from the barley stubble it is better to eat than any sort of bird a man may shoot for his dinner. This was discovered when man had nothing better to shoot with than a bow and arrow.

A Fowler's World

When the cold wind whispers in the reeds it may not reach the sheltering fowl in the water down below, but a steady fall in temperature puts a layer of ice on the pond or flash, stiffens the mud in open places and drives the duck to feed where it might otherwise never be seen. It is saddening to see the ultimate false tameness induced by conservation of energy and a lowering of vitality. When it is well nourished the duck springs from the water and climbs into the sky with power, skims down over the lake, makes a circuit and comes back in again all in a few seconds or at the most a minute or two, but as the hard weather continues the bird's survival begins to depend on the minimum exertion. It is slow to rise, sluggish on the wing, a prey to the sharpened fox, the falcon, the crow, the big black-headed gulls that wait about like undertakers.

A Fowler's World

The slope of a barley field can look like the tousled head of a boy newly risen from bed – except that it can never be straightened again. The knives of the binder will crop the heads and they will tumble to the ground, the combine will drag the straw by its roots and men will have to take time to clear the great harvesting machine of clods of grass and soil and tangled straw. A good malting barley is a precious crop. Distillers and brewers buy the grain before it has sprouted but he is a lucky man who cuts a whole field without losing a bushel or two, even in a summer when the sun shines and the corn is cut with little loss of time. The barley field attracts more than the contractor and the combine team. It lures the birds. Partridges and pheasants walk through the fallen corn and fill their crops, and at nightfall – the ducks come.

A Fowler's World

Greylags marked the day like the creamery whistle and the distant train. People would take out their watches and check the hour after they heard the whistle, the train and the geese. Ploughmen on the high hill would look away across the moorland and remark on the morning flight of greylags. It was time for tea and scones to be brought to the field, the scones to be unwrapped from newspaper and the hot tea poured into a bowl while the ploughman crouched on his heels and admired the geese steadily sailing in to the winds of the river, babbling and circling and sinking lower and lower until they touched down on the meadows with a last flash of white underwing and an abrupt ending of their melodic conversation.

A Fowler's World

In the morning, as the cutting begins, the ground vibrates with the giant tread of the Clydesdales. The song of the grasshopper population is drowned by the clatter and rattle of wheels and running binder sheets. The mechanical arms cast out sheaves when the knotter and the knife have done their work, the work of hands. The butts of the sheaves are filled with the succulent green life that fed rabbits, sheltered the mouse. Everything on the fringe creeps deeper into the field. The five feet at the headland becomes five yards, fifty yards. The partridges creep out at midday when the horses are led home for a trough of corn and a drink at the water-hole. They hurry off through the stubble, past lying sheaves in stooks, to finally throw themselves up into the air and sail over the dike. A rabbit, isolated out there by that ring of tramping hooves and a noise like the end of the world, bolts for the ditch and the warren, but the mouse knows no other world but the vastness of the clover and the grass beneath the tall trees of the oats. The pheasant hen has done what she will do in the open field or in the wood, she has crouched in a hollow, trusting to her camouflage to protect her. When the knives are close she will run out and launch herself in flight, accompanied by her nearest neighbour. The small boy playing in the stooks will catch a vole and search vainly for the shrew after he has heard its shrill and frantic warning. In three or four days the grasshoppers and beetles providing a grand banquet for the birds that come between cutting and carting.

The very nature of harvest gives the life of the field time to recover. The corn ripens and dries in the sheaf. Another field has to be cut while cutting weather holds. The great change in the cut-down forest becomes accepted. The mouse runs warily and the rabbit pops across the ditch, for there is a tasty bite in the undergrowth. The owls hunt when the sun has gone from the western sky and the field sits sleeping. The habits of the field have changed. Once the mouse and the shrew were safe and ran about their world when the sun was up, but now they are back to life as it is when the corn is shorn, and their habits are nocturnal. Even the pheasant is on the stubble at sunset and sunrise, together with the rabbits and the journeying hare, for who can say to what field or hill – for that matter to what man – a hare belongs.

This thing would happen annually on the hills that were under corn, the Low Planting Hill, the Other Clutag Hill, the Big Hill and the Switchback Hill. The low fields, too, saw this change, but on two of the hills, those adjoining the moss, when the corn was cut, the grouse came. Harvest was always after the shooting began on the far moss, often in late

August. The grouse and black game were fond of a feed from the stooks and announced their arrival night and morning with the cry that was normally only heard up in the peat moss, away on the road to the farthest hills and the rocks above the sea.

Pastures New

The grouse came to the road as they always do. They needed grit to digest their food. The few times they were shot was when poachers waited for them to come for the grit. The road was watched by keepers of adjoining moors, who knew well that if they marked the cross-roads after hearing a shot they stood a good chance of identifying or catching the culprits. Grouse, even the grouse that lived on Clanty Moss, were wary on open ground without cover at hand. Anyone walking up the grey road could count on seeing the grouse moving ahead, slipping away into the heather and showing themselves no more. Only a poacher prepared to lie up in an alder clump or a damp ditch could hope to shoot the birds on the road and not even then, unless he was very lucky, could he reckon on bagging more than one. Once a shot was fired the keepers were alerted and the whole of the moorland listened and watched.

Grouse nest early in the year. Young grouse are often drowned when peat holes and drains are flooded. The hen leads them on from one place to another. It is imperative that she does so because they are always in danger from predators, and food is nowhere plentiful. The tallest heather buds out of reach of chicks and by the end of July they must all be able to fend for themselves. The whole moor has a short summer, a short breeding season. On the fringes it

seems that the bracken is hardly up before it loses its bright green and begins to age. The heather may be slow to show colour, but in an incredibly short time it will lose its lustre, bleach and die. The adder sleeps only a few weeks on the mounds of fine grass. Summer is late and short. When the apples are ripening in lowland gardens and the damson is drooping with fruit-laden boughs, the moorland rowan's berries are already crimson and the leaves touched with rust.
The Way of a Countryman

There is a blueness among the firs and the pigeons seem to vanish into its depths, enveloping and safe.
Fresh Woods

Tread softly, for there are stones buried along the grass and the sound of your boot on a stone would make an echo up in the trees.
Fresh Woods

The poacher is on the far side of the field, a figure hard to see, for he is standing close to the oak tree with a hawthorn behind him. He did not see the pheasants go off the field. He looked for them within yards of the spot on which they fed, but his eye caught the pigeon gliding out over the fringe of the wood and he saw it loop up and go in the fast flight back in the direction from which it came. It was all too far away for him to have seen the keeper or his dogs, or for the pigeon to have sighted him by the oak tree, although the pigeon has keener eyes than the hawk. The pigeon was no

more than a dot. To the man who has not studied the char-
acteristic flight of birds it might have looked like a pigeon,
a crow, a magpie or even a fieldfare. Its turn in flight from a
glide to fast beating wings could have indicated a hundred
things and none of them the right thing, but the poacher
knew in that instant where the keeper stood, and the keeper knew too, when he heard the clatter of the pigeon's
wings, that if the pigeon had been observed, the poacher was
moving away with the same noiseless stealth as the pheasants.

The poaching of a pheasant by day is a thing of great
stealth or great speed. The wind is blowing and making the
whole wood rock. It has blown since the earliest hours of
the morning. The crossed limbs of an ash and gangling thorn
squeak and groan, and dead fir cones rain on the grass and
path. The pigeons, carried across the undulating country by
the buffeting wind, sweep in and take bobbing foothold on
the top branches of tall trees from which they can keep
watch. They are more nervous because in the wind the
warning is carried away unheard. They love the hollow still-
ness of the watery sunset when the smallest noise resounds
through the drum of the wood. Now they sway aloft there
until they tire of the vigilance and take a short heavy flight
to the sea of thick fir-tops.

The Poacher's Handbook

. . . and the Ways of Fish and Fishermen

The way to the hills isn't easy but one must go to remote
places if one is to have peace and to learn the way of wild
trout, catching them in spite of all the difficulties that beset
a fisherman in such places.

Trout from the Hills

However few were the fish in this bit of water, which in places flowed out and deserved the name of stream, and in others narrowed and became a ditch, it began my interest in fishing. Here I cornered a minnow in my cupped palms, here I watched the snaking progress of the eel, marvelling at its gracefulness in the sun-heated water. In this place I stood and stared at the waterhen taking flight with trailing feet, going hastily up to the narrows and making a little furrow in the slow current, a thing that spread out in delicate ripples and vanished before it lapped the banks. The biggest eel I ever saw moved in this stream. It came as I slumped over the wall gazing into the water, and it moved idly, waving its broad tail for all the world like the leaf of a submerged flag, except that it was brown and partly transparent, instead of opaque like the green leaf. I could have speared him with a fork, but I watched while he crossed the sun-kissed patch between a great slab of rock and a few round boulders. I was very small. It was a wonderful thing and thrilled me as only the lightening dart of a trout could thrill me after. I enjoyed the moment or two just as I later enjoyed the sight of the first brown trout I ever caught, marvelling at the beauty of its colouring, the marking of its dark back, so well matched to the bed of the stream, the shade of its under-side, cream, tea rose, honeysuckle, the shade of the belly of the stoat.

The Poacher's Handbook

The eel lives under a slab of stone. Most of the day it lives in the recess beneath the stone, but when the sun is on the water, or some special flavour is in the stream, it moves out and goes weaving along to burrow into a little mound of mud. The mud streams in discolouration and the eel finds its food in the mud, taking the beetle or the larva of the fly, a

hunter in the eerie world of muddied water. After a while it
returns to its sheltering stone, backing into its home until
only the tip of its head protrudes. When the heron comes
stalking along the burn, the eel's head will be withdrawn.
The heron will stand there waiting his time, patient as only
a master angler can be patient. There is no morning, noon
or night when this happens, only hunger and the chances of
survival. If the heron is to survive he must take his eel or
trout fry or vole somewhere along the burn's course. If the
eel is to survive he must remain beneath his protecting slab
of rock. The heron waits, the eel waits, just as the hunting cat
sits endlessly above the home of the mouse.

Pastures New

Just as there are haunts of rabbits, fox, badger and every other
sort of land animal, there are haunts of different kinds of fish.

Ian Niall's Complete Angler

. . . the pike is mysterious, snake-like, primeval and secret in
its habits and habitat, even though one may see him dozing
among the reeds on a hot summer's afternoon, his lithe body
barely covered by the water.

The Way of a Countryman

Come and see the geds, they said to me a long time ago
when I looked down at a great pool at the bend in the river,
and down I went to look at the pike that occasionally shot
through the lesser fish shoaling on the edge of the reeds.
There are faster fish, of course. The pike has only a sudden
burst of speed that enables him to overtake his prey. He

needs only this. Once he comes up with it the end is certain. Nine times out of ten he takes another fish crosswise in his jaws and then turns and swallows it head-first, but the tenth time he takes it from the tail and can't let go and I have had this happen often when bringing a small pike in and have landed two instead of one.

The pike in the river were big enough, but there were bigger pike, I was told, in dozens of quiet water-holes and lakes. Some were big enough to take a child by the arm and drag it into the water. Some could bolt a pheasant or a wild duck that the gunner brought down. There had been one, away over the hills yonder, that had been longer than the keeper who caught it and its tail had dragged on the ground while he carried it home slung over his shoulder. Small boys fished for these monsters with anything they could find for bait. A dead rat from the rickyard, a kitten drowned in the rain-barrel, a frog, a mouse, a bit of pork, a strip of red flannel, the guts of a chicken. Keepers sometimes used wire fastened to the fence posts and threw out great conger-eel tackles to hold monsters. People who took them from the river were honour-bound to kill them. A lot of them fed their pike to the hens after boiling them in a setpot or cauldron.

The Way of a Countryman

The bittern, a bird that sometimes haunts the fen in which the pike swims, is known as a 'down-looker'. Its eyes are so placed in his skull that when it seems to be looking over the marsh it is actually watching the water immediately below its beak.

The pike then, is an 'up-looker'. His eyes are so placed in his skull that he looks towards the surface of the water. He sees what passes above, rather than beneath him. He looks like the green weeds and the dapples of sunlight seen on the bottom.

Ian Niall's Complete Angler

There is a time when summer is young and the wagtails are nesting by the water, when the flow of the stream slackens and the rocks begin to show. The pools here and there become shallow and the sound of the water dies and the man after a fish forgets how it frothed in colour when the spate of spring roared through the hollows and licked at the top of the bridge's arc. When the water only whispers and sighs and bubbles among the stones the boy from the cottage will come and lie on his stomach and watch the trout. In a little while he will begin dabbling his arms in the water, having dragged his sleeves almost up to his shoulders.

Watch him. He is at the old game of tickling a trout. His hands go feeling in under the belly of the rock. He knows the places where the biggest trout shelter. If you learn to tickle trout you will learn to move your hands in the way you reach a ferret, without an excited jerky movement. Smoothly, confidently. The trout, speckled brown and with a cream shade on its under-side almost a match for the delicate old tea rose, will remain motionless, or almost motionless; a gentle movement of the gills and the slightest balancing against the cold water coming down from the hills. At the coming of the searching fingers he will edge forward a fraction, aware, a little uneasy perhaps, but sure in his knowledge that one movement of his tail and fins and he will be off through the pool as fast as the brief reflection of the flying swallow. The hands of the boy are guided by his eyes. He lies sprawled over the rock. One violent motion and he might find himself head first in the pool, but the fingers spread and draw close to the trout. The fish floats higher, closer to the rock. Now the fingers gently reach the underside of the fish and caress the slipperiness. The trout backs a little. The fingers stroke again and the trout edges back, nervously now, ready to dart away, and the boy waits his time. Now the trout has retreated until the gills are above the fingers and the hands take sudden hold in the only spot a hand can grip and retain a living fish in water. Now the trout is up in the air and its life going fast in gulps and a frantic jerking of its tail.

This is the way of tickling trout. Before you become a hand at it you will have many a wetting and lose a dozen or so, but the ragged boy from the village school would make a fine teacher.

The Poacher's Handbook

Ask about flies and they will tell you the secrets of the old fly-tiers.

Trout from the Hills

Fishing the wet fly produces more fish than dry fly-fishing, particularly in lakes where the wind is often gusty, the water disturbed, and the clouds often obscure the sun for considerable periods. The dry fly needs a moderate ripple or, indeed, no ripple at all, so long as the surface tension will support a greased line. It also needs a degree of sunlight to enable the feeding trout to pick out the morsel on the surface. An inch or two makes all the difference to a feeding fish. The dry fly is, or should be, on top of the water. The wet fly jerks and twitches an inch or two beneath the surface where it can be readily seen. Imagine a fly moving beneath a skylight window as opposed to one on top of the glass, and then consider the glass obscured to a degree by the dark clouds that may cross the sun.

Trout from the Hills

Why a black fly? It can hardly be denied that a large number of black or very dark flies are to be found in country where the land and the lake beds are peaty and dark.

Without going into a long list of black flies I might say that the sedge family contributes many of the blacks and dark-hued flies. Many beetles that swim in the water and move on the surface are black; the lake olive is a dark-bodied fly; the buzzing blue-bottle is as near black as makes no difference; the family of midges and mosquitoes contribute not a few dark flies. My black fly with its greeny hackle served to cover the green-bottle, the blow-fly, and the giant Welsh-fly with death and decay in its Latin name. I fished it and watched trout come to it in preference to live sedges on the water. I stood more than once to see a trout select this black fly from a host of others because it was a shade bigger and perhaps looked meatier. I cast to the rise with it, drifted it, fished it through the ripple in fits and starts and the trout smashed at it. All the best lake trout I have caught have been taken on this fly.

Trout from the Hills

Take Davy, for instance. He was the best tier of flies in the town of B. He could tie a fly for any lake, and they will tell

you that different flies are to be used on every lake. A black
fly does well on this one, but you must have a touch of red
for the lake over the hill; and the beetle, if it is fished at such
and such lake, must always have a tail, while a tail never does
any good at the lake down below. Davy was tying flies one
night in the winter. Unlike some of the other fly-tiers of B,
Davy had a skill at imitating natural insects and went in for
this branch of the art more than for homespun flies designed
to catch trout. One of the flies he tied on this occasion was
to the pattern of a freshly killed green bottle-fly which he
had obtained from somewhere. The fly being completed, he
laid it on the table beside the natural one to compare his
work with that of the Creator. At that instant a spider came
on the table, ran quickly across it and made off with Davy's
newly-tied fly, scorning the natural one. What chance would
a fish have against Davy's art, I ask you?

You may smile at this story. It was told me very solemnly.
Trout from the Hills

Time had added many inches to that fish. He has become as
fat as a pig ready for the bacon market. He has brightened
with the passing of years. His spots have become more magnificent, his mouth more gaping, his gills redder. I hesitate to
say how big he is or how much he weighs now, but more
than thirty years ago I suppose he was six ounces and not
many inches more than six. You will understand this if you
are a fisherman born, if the poetry of it was in you from
childhood.
Trout from the Hills

The sun glints on the dark grey muds of a slow-flowing

canal or lake and here, in the deeps, swim bream. The bream searches the muds for the pea mussel, the water slater, which is something like the dry-land wood louse, worms and larvae as well as snails. The common bream is a wonderful golden brown or bronze. He is deep-bodied. His mouth is specially designed for sifting the mud to extract the larvae of midges called bloodworms.

The bream will feed standing on his head and waving his tail as he takes in mud and blows it out again. He might be called a riverbed scavenger. In winter he prefers the deeps and, as always, seeks the company of his own kind.
Ian Niall's Complete Angler

Let me talk of the lakes that have poetic names. The well of the frog, and the lake of the moon, the servant's well and the black lake, the lake of the bird and the lake of the hound, the lake of the mill and the lake of the bare mountain. Not every one has a good trout in it, lest you have a map and a knowledge of Welsh to help you trace the location. Some contain bright little fish that hardly ever rise, and in some the fish move only at certain times and the common catch is but one or two fish as a reward for a whole day's fishing. How big is a big mountain-lake trout? I have seen one or two that could have been salmon but for the fact that no salmon could ascend so far. A good lake trout is a fish that would grace a glass case, one of three to four pounds perhaps, with a bit of kelp to make him look old and fierce. If the good lake trout is to lie on my plate at supper with molten butter running down its skin it need be no more than three-quarters of a pound, and half a pound will do. They say that the little fish of a quarter of a pound is better eating, but a lot of little fish are not young and tender, but dwarfed by the lack of food and condition. Let the table trout be half to three-quarters of a pound and let it be firm and pink, for there is no more delicately flavoured trout than a pink-fleshed one.

Trout from the Hills

The way to the hills isn't easy but one must go to remote places if one is to have peace and to learn the way of wild trout, catching them in spite of all the difficulties that beset a fisherman in such places. The mountain challenges man. Some climb mountains simply to say they have climbed them and a few, a very few, look for yesterday and a sort of timelessness that is to be found in places that haven't changed since man walked the earth. In the heart of the hills, hidden by a shoulder or cradled in rocks there may be an acre or two of deep, cold water where the mountain trout are to be found. Not all mountain trout are large. Most, in fact, are small and hardly worth fishing for, but some are big. Some live on their own kind and grow yet bigger. Some are fed by minnows in summer and never look at a fly. Some cruise in the dark and rise, once in a while, to a moth or some other fluttering insect that dimples and disturbs the water.

To begin with, the mountain lake fisherman must have imagination. He must have imagination and a stout heart. He must dream a little and know how things are up there in the blue mist of evening when the sun is going down. Far off in the shelter of his town and village, he may imagine that the tarn in the hills sits in sunshine and that the fish go round and round in great circles, rising as regularly as the minutes tick by, that the water is like a sheet of glass and that midges dance and the nightjar calls. It isn't often so. Once in a season this may be. The magic of a summer's evening may be upon that far-off place, the golden sunshine may glint on the rocks as the last rays of the light of day strike the high peaks, and down below, where the great boulders stand about the water, the place may be enchanted and all the big trout that ever moved up and out of the deeps may be feeding while on the lonely mountain the ewe bleats and her lamb answers. The man who goes to find this magic finds it sooner or later, in a season, two seasons, three. He finds, in the passing of his days, that the mountain has a strange character of its own. It sulks, it broods, it breathes a cold, damp breath upon him when the daylight is dying and the ewe coughs or the wild mountain fox barks, and the place has an enchantment that is disturbing, while the feeders that tumble off the rocks and make a churning of fresh water where they join the lake are talking softly to each other; or are the spirits of dead men there, whispering as the shadows deepen? When the trout rises on the black mirror of the lake in shadow the fisherman has lost heart. It is time to go home and speak to flesh and blood men, down below in the valley, in the warmth of familiar places. He dare not speak to himself lest some spirit join in and answer.

Trout from the Hills

The climb began shortly after we had met the quarrymen as they got down from the milk lorry. They waved us on, saying that no matter how we climbed there would be plenty of time to fish when we got there. My friend and I set off eagerly, plodding through the rocks and scrambling upwards. Half-an-hour later, having discovered that each new skyline appearing had been set back there to lure us to burst our hearts and lungs with renewed efforts to reach our destination, we sat down on a great slab of stone and looked back at the two quarrymen coming slowly up behind us. My hands were shaking, my legs trembling and heart pounding in my throat, or so it seemed. My companion was ready to lie down and forgo the pleasure of ever getting to the top.

'I'm done!' he gasped. 'I only want to recover and get back home. I don't care if I never see the lake and never fish again.'

To be truthful, I had almost reached the same state. I began to wonder if the quarrymen were real. Was the whole thing an illusion? Were we in the company of ghosts? Ghosts, however don't stop to eat a bit of bread and cheese and call out that they came without their breakfasts in case they missed the lorry and disappointed us. My companion groaned at this. Disappointed! He wished they had had their breakfasts and forgotten us. He was still sitting on the rock when they plodded past him, smiling gently and reassuring him that it wasn't far now, only about another three hundred feet up, fifteen minutes and no more. You didn't see the lake until you were right at it. That was the thing that took the steam out of you. I waited for my companion to get to his feet. He looked utterly beaten.

'I don't believe it', he muttered. 'There is no such place. They invented it. It doesn't exist!'

The quarrymen had vanished behind the next outcrop of rock. I caught his arm and urged him to make haste. In two or three minutes we were too out of breath to complain any more. We needed all our wind to keep climbing. This, we were told, was the lake of the moon.

The lake of the moon probably got its name because it sits

up in the mountains as high as the moon. It is a shallow lake and the earliest lake I know. Shallow lakes are generally warmer in spring than deep waters, plant life recovers sooner. When these conditions exist trout will come into condition all the sooner. Will rise early in the season. The lake of the moon is such a place. Lakes at the same altitude are often deeper. Where the water is deep the fish go down in winter to escape the colder layers of water nearest to the surface. They are slow to come up out of the depths, slow to come into condition and such lakes are known as late lakes. The early lakes have usually one other special advantage. They are rich in daphnia, one of the secrets of lakes that appear to have good trout without a particularly good hatch of flies even in the best part of summer. High lakes that have good trout either have a considerable area of weed and plant life to shelter and sustain insects, or some rich bottom-feeding in the shape of beetles, which, with the caddis and the sedge which emerges from it, make a good part of the diet of wild lake trout.

In the lake of the moon we fished while our hosts watched. They had made the climb and given their sport over to us out of good fellowship. The fish we caught they would not share although a week before, seeing us cold and blue by that lake in the valley, they had both offered us part of their catch.

Trout from the Hills

Willie got down at the gate and sniffed, rose, ran a few paces and got down again. I followed. I was impressed. Here was a hunter, a discoverer of lost pigs.

Fresh Woods

Spring got in Tom's blood. He watched the peewits, the curlews and the oyster-catchers that often made nests on the field. Later he watched the partridges and pheasants with equal success. He made many a shilling delivering the eggs of the latter to the keeper.

Pastures New

2
Characters: Fact and Fiction

THE FIRST HEROES OF MY YOUNG LIFE were ploughmen and byremen, strong fellows who were apparently fearless, simple men who sat and talked in the stable, talked about the way of birds in the woods and the animals in the fields. They talked of other things, of course, things that I quickly came to understand to be the simple facts of life, the ways of servant-girls and their willingness or otherwise to be persuaded to climb drystone walls and roll in the sweet-smelling grass, their facility to produce unwanted 'weans' and ask for impossible sums of money to maintain little strangers! Ten shillings was an impossible sum, a fearful price to pay for an hour in the hay, for a man might earn no more than ten shillings a week and his keep. A byreman 'waged' for ten shillings. A ploughman was a pound, especially if he milked as well. Good men were hard to find and lazy fellows it seemed were more numerous than crows. Many good men left the countryside to try their hand at farming in Canada and some, perhaps, took to their heels when their work in the hayfield bore fruit.

In the main our men were respectable, some of them sons of farmers themselves, and not a few of them morally upright and much less hypocritical in their conduct than the elders of the kirk. There was John who carried me after dinner astride his neck all the way to the stable, a ritual that was only broken when there happened to be a downpour of rain. I worshipped John. No one displayed more bravery than he did when a great

Clydesdale came rushing up past the midden hauling a cart of corn and threatening to slip and overturn the lot and perhaps crush John between the cartwheel and the wall of the byre. He could hold restive horses, sitting back on his heels with his legs braced, and he did it all without cursing the way some plough-men did. He talked to horses the way they should be talked to, and there was never a moment when his heroic image was tar-nished in my sight. John True was his proper name, or perhaps this is my romantic recollection of him, the tallest, straightest, kindest of all the men who worked for Grandfather.

A Galloway Childhood

Willie

WE ALL HAVE OUR DREAMS, and Willie was no exception. He came to work for my grandfather as his ploughman and that is how we met. Every Sunday, as soon as he had finished his work, he would gather his things together and ride off home on a bicycle, his weekly washing tied in a brown paper parcel on the carrier. His parents had one of the 'wee crofts' tucked away on a back road that real-ly led nowhere. It was one of those places that was too small for a man with a family, and too big for one who had no other help.

Willie had left home to work while his brother Tam stayed at home to help his father. Life was far from easy and Willie longed to get away from the land altogether, although he had never seen a city or mingled in a crowd bigger than that at the market or cattle show. I used to talk to Willie a lot, plodding along beside him while he ploughed, and some-times distracting him to look at a nest on the ground or along the bank. He talked about the world beyond the horizon and baffled me with his longing to go there when I knew it was a world of grime and noise and continual bustle, a world in which the idlers lined the pavements and the well-off rode in taxicabs, the idlers looking grey-faced and gaunt and the well-off as smooth as baconers, and twice as fat. Why anyone who could listen to the peewit calling and see the partridges swinging round to land wanted to enter such a world was beyond me, but Willie did.

Willie wanted the locomotion and the smell of cigar smoke, even if he couldn't afford the cigar. He would walk with a silver-mounted walking stick and wear shoes of shining patent leather, looking far smarter than any farmer at a wedding or a funeral. Willie talked to me about the world he dreamed of and I talked to him of the world that filled my mind. The small boy in Willie responded to my questions about where the heron nested and where the burn began. These were the wonders of my world as he had dreams of tramcars and clanging bells and, above all else, a gleaming motor cycle that would take him everywhere at great speed.

The Idler's Companion

Snib

LET ME SHOW YOU SNIB, for I cannot undertake to introduce you. Snib is a close character. He hangs about the bridge until the public-house opens in the morning. He spits tobacco juice into the river while he waits for opening time in the evening. He has very little to say. When the cormorant bobs and dives again he watches it with detached interest. Perhaps he is making an idle bet with himself as to where it will rise, or perhaps he is absorbed in scratching the hair below his cap. He completes the scene for the visitor. There is always a man looking at a river on a sunny afternoon, watching the whorls of water, the fragments of vegetable and animal life that spin and glide under the bridge and out towards the estuary. Snib makes the scene complete, but he doesn't watch the water for the bubbles and the whorls. He watches for the salmon coming up. When the tide runs out he will take note of the obstacles revealed at low water and when it is dark he will remember.

Stand close to the bar and hear him whisper, 'A nice fish for tomorrow?' When he speaks of fish he means only one fish, the salmon. He and his son have a net and a boat and no conscience or love for the bailiff. In the dark Snib will remember what he saw in the afternoon, the tree branch that had bedded itself in the sand below the bend, the tangle of wire collecting weed and rubbish just at the bend. He and his son will wrap rag round the oars, put the net into the boat and paddle themselves down the water in a darkness like the crow's wing. When they are past the bend, the wire obstacle and the submerged tree, they will draw to the bank, stake down the net and then row silently across the water. Snib will feed out the net. The weighted side will sink and the other will float, supported by the corks along its edge. The running tide will belly the net and the salmon, swimming with the current, will come to the meshes. In a little while, and without more than a whisper between them, Snib and his son will row back, drawing the net in a sweep to the other bank. Snib will step ashore and his son will follow him, dropping anchor while he gives a hand. The salmon will be big enough if they are eight to twelve pounds in weight. One netting will be enough. It is a dangerous game, for there is a regulation about a licence and another about the size of the mesh of the net, as well as the number of fish that may be taken.

In the morning Snib will be at the kitchen door asking if he can have a word with the hotel keeper or his wife. Something about a salmon at twelve or thirteen shillings a pound and as fresh as the morning.

The Poacher's Handbook

Francie

ON MY FIRST EXPEDITION with the long net I was helper to Francie. He is a bold character. A long time ago he was chased by a keeper who fired a shot at him. The pellets of lead entered Francie's neck. They did no more than raise a few beads of blood. Some were hooked out by Francie's mother with a darning needle. The others remained. Francie is quite proud of them and he will ask you to feel them as they roll under his skin at the pressure of your finger, saying, 'Number four shot, them. Enough there to bring down a goose!' On another occasion, running at full speed down a ride in the wood, he tripped over a stretched wire and sprawled on his face. A second wire, set close to the first, cut him across the bridge of his nose. The injury so infuriated Francie that he waited for his pursuer and laid him low with the butt of his gun.

Francie and I took stable lanterns. A lighted lantern shows for miles, but we were on the secluded side of a wood and in the shelter of a hill. These lanterns were Francie's bravado. It is safer to work with a flash-lamp or a small lamp of some kind, for the storm lantern shows for miles when it has to be carried along the net so that the rabbits are dazzled and can be lifted quickly. I knew Francie hoped for some kind of excitement. We had three dozen rabbits at the first setting and had them in a sack and the net rolled, ready for moving on, when we heard a stone fall from a dyke. Francie stood out from the shelter of the wood, his outline a dark patch on the grey of the field.

'Haste you down the woodside an' away,' he whispered.

Groaning under my burden, I staggered off with the sack, the net and the sticks. Behind me Francie stood like a post in the field. Once I was safely on the road I put the net and the sack in the ditch and sat down to wait. Francie joined me in half an hour. He had walked round the keeper twice, he said, and had half thought of lighting the lantern I had left behind. I was thankful to get home that night.

The Poacher's Handbook

Little Hugh

LITTLE HUGH GATHERS MUSHROOMS and fire-wood. It enables him to watch and take note. He does a bit of hedging and ditching. He can manage an isolated burrow with three nets and a ferret while he is trimming and bending the sticks of a hedge. The ferret travels in his jacket pocket, as tame as the old spinster's cat. Little Hugh can take his old gun along with his ditching tools, the sickle, the mattock, the draining shovel and the hedge-knife. If the pheasant, feeding where the old corn stack once stood, ventures a little nearer the ditch, Hugh will take one shot after he has stared idly around for ten minutes or so. He can move very fast for a man of sixty. Up out of the ditch, through the wire and over to the bird and back almost before the echo has returned to the hill.

Someone comes down the field, suspicious of Little Hugh, perhaps, but the pheasant is on the bank covered by a tangle of green weed, blackberry and uprooted cress. A shot? Surprise at finding someone standing so close shows on Little Hugh's face. Yes, he heard a shot not so long ago and wondered about it too. Is the keeper on his rounds? Who could be shooting at this time of the day? The old gun is lying down in the ditch, balanced on three stones close to the bank. Stand clear. Small pebbles and marshy grit come swinging up on the shovel. A dog is barking the cows home. Little Hugh adjusts his cap and feels the farthest corner of his buttonless waistcoat's pocket. When the stump of a ciga-rette is smouldering in his sheltering palm he calls to the departing visitor. Is it nearly tea time?

The Poacher's Handbook

Black Bill

BLACK BILL WAS ALEADY an old man when I was a child. I remember meeting him, or passing him at any rate, when I was being walked home from the 'preaching' at the country school-house one Sunday evening in early summer. My aunts had a firm belief that a preaching was a good thing for a small boy, if it only taught him to sit still and keep quiet for an hour and a half, and hard it was to seem attentive to the preacher when, behind the school-house the pigeons called through the wood, and close by its door ran a singing stream.

'Here's that character, Black Bill!' one whispered to the

other as they hurried me along.

'He's a bit like Jesus,' I said solemnly as I took note of that character, and indeed he might well have been an apostle, for he had large soulful eyes and a curly black beard.

'Think shame!' my aunts scolded in unison and averted their gaze when we passed Black Bill.

I looked at him and he smiled; then all at once I lost his attention, for he switched his regard to a greenfinch that flew up and seemed to throw itself over the hedge. My boots squeaked as I plodded homeward. After a while I turned my head and looked back. Black Bill was hanging about a watering hole at the side of the road and probably observing a waterhen I had noticed there as we had hurried past.

'Well,' I said quietly to assuage the shocked religious feelings of my elders, 'if he is not like Jesus he's a bit like John the Baptist!'

'He's a good-for-nothing old poacher!' said one of them.

'He's a dirty old tramp!' added the other, 'and he catches little goldfinches and sells them, and the Lord will punish him!'

'He looked like the Lord to me,' I said.

For the rest of the journey home through the gathering dusk, under the ash trees, through the floating clouds of midges and up the footpath and over the stile until we came to the whitewashed farm with its peat smoke going up to the night, I heard the history of Black Bill, disciple of the devil, so they said.

Black Bill was a man for birds, they told me. He just naturally went after any kind of bird; bantams of Willie Adair, the fowls of the schoolmistress, the guinea birds of Mrs McQuade, the little bird that sang in the tree and worst of all, the pheasants and partridges in every wood and field for miles and miles.

'He's an ill character,' they wound up as we reached the farm kitchen, 'the like of which we wouldn't have about the place. Your grandmother once lost a set of turkey eggs through Black Bill, the villain! Your grandfather encouraged him here, to spite the gamekeeper for something they had fallen out about, but he was glad to see the back of him, we can tell you!'

My grandfather had been dozing by the fire. He sat up and lit his pipe, running a spill quickly through his fingers to quench its flame as he always did.

'Black Bill?' he said. 'Black Bill can charm a bird off a tree. He has the way of such things. He keeps a whistle in his pocket and when he's near a bird he plays a bit of a tune, I've heard.'

'He sounds a gentle man,' I ventured.

My grandfather laughed.

'A black-hearted, wild savage!' said one of my aunts coming from down the hall, where she had been to hang her coat.

It was a long time before I got to know the truth of Black Bill, the man who could charm the little bird. I did not see him again for ten years or more. By that time I had taken to mooching the hedges with an old gun and had had the lessons of Francie and Little Hugh to add to those of Jeck.

There is a time, just after the harvest, when the ground seems shorn, yet green with exposed clover; when the hare is uncovered and runs in the sight of man and the partridge coveys are scattered more often. On autumn days, before the first cold wind comes, the poacher begins to take note of the movement of the partridges, listens to the 'two-thri' call they make at nightfall and thinks about the net and the gun. I had been walking through a field of roots, hoping to put up partridges, and came to the hedge above the road. My heart bounded when I suddenly knew I was being watched, and then relief came when I realised that the watcher was not my enemy, the keeper. I looked at Black Bill. He stood in a gateway, his hands thrust deeply into the pockets of his over-large jacket, his black head and beard a tousled tangle. I went to the gate and bade him good afternoon.

'I was looking for a partridge,' I said

'A partridge?' He fumbled in his pocket and brought out a brass whistle made from the ends of two cartridges.

'Two-thri, two-thri, two-thri,' he whistled.

It was the call of the partridge collecting covey, rasping, pausing and beginning again, the sound that was somehow dusk and the pathetic bleating of sheep when the last glow of sun had gone off the highest hill. Black Bill's lips parted and showed remarkably white teeth while he whistled. Now he turned and swung his arms up, quietly pointing over the field. I caught my breath. Out of the ragged furrows of turnips a partridge ventured, inquisitive; a foot raised and held up, then delicately put down on the dusty earth; a movement through the motionless leaves and the straggling sorrel and another of the covey followed the first. They stood near each other, necks a little stretched, immaculate and beautiful little brown birds. I could only watch. I was no longer the poacher after a partridge. Black Bill looked at me. I shook my head silently. He put his hand to his mouth and removed the whistle from his teeth. The two partridges stood there. I could have killed them, but I could only think of what I had heard of Black Bill, who could lure birds.

'Shoot them,' he said softly. 'A black-hearted savage,' I heard my aunt say.

'I couldn't,' I said and my voice frightened the birds, for

they then ran quickly up the furrow as soon as I spoke.

'I couldn't kill a partridge either,' said Black Bill. 'I could have shot hundreds in my time, thousands, yes!'

'I couldn't shoot them when they come like that,' I said, for I had my conscience and I had shot and eaten my share.

'A partridge to some,' said Black Bill, 'is just a little snack on a plate with gravy runnin' round it.'

'I've heard you're a bird catcher,' I said.

He grinned through his whiskers. 'The partridge is the one bird I don't touch,' he said; 'but the old pheasant – now there's a proud an' impudent bird. I never spared one yet!'

We walked along the road together and he let me see his whistle. It was no more than an ordinary cartridge-case whistle, the kind of thing a poacher makes for his son to pass the time in the evening, and takes from him again in a day or two because the incessant noise is driving the family insane! I tried it with poor results. Black Bill explained that it wanted a great deal of practice. As we walked, the cry of a partridge came to us across a dun field of raked stubble. He put the whistle in his mouth and begun to make notes. It needed sharp eyesight to see the covey gathering. We stood a long time while the countryside fell asleep. The partridges came across the stubble, nearer and nearer to us, then Black Bill suddenly clapped his hands and they sank into the cover of the stalks.

The Poacher's Handbook

Danny

DANNY WAS A STURDY LITTLE MAN, past middle age and unmarried. He had lost both his parents when the house they were living in burnt down. Thereafter he was brought up by his mother's sister. She still looked after him, even when he came back from the war, and he took his washing back to her every other week-end when he had a day and night off. Danny loved birds and I loved them too. Whenever the opportunity presented itself he would take me to watch the swallows as they flitted in and out of the cart shed where they nested on the beams. We watched the waterhen walking on the ooze beyond the byre midden and more than once ran to catch a second glimpse of the corncrake that would cross the wee field, the home paddock behind the steading to get to the hayfield beyond. There was, I am sure, a particular innocence about Danny that hardly anyone else appreciated.

The peacock catastrophe came upon us when, one weekend as he was tying his washing on his battered bike, Danny looked at me and winked and said, 'I'm going to get you a peacock, son, but you'll promise not to say a word?' I promised.

Feathered Friends

Paddy

THE PICNIC WAS THE HIGHLIGHT of summer. Everyone helped to prepare. Everyone hurried though the essential chores that were the price of those few hours in the tangy air of the sea on a shore as peaceful and drowsy as our own back hills where nothing happened but the singing of the lark ascending from the clover.

It was on one of these trips that I was taken to meet Paddy. Grandfather had been known to spend almost the whole Sunday sitting in Paddy's cave talking to him about the great days of long ago, the year of the short corn and famine, or the big snow.

I can remember going into Paddy's 'garden' because he stopped working along his potato rows and came to open the gate so that we could come in. The gate was a heavy iron affair with twine hinges attaching it to a weathered post. It served to keep wandering animals such as sheep out of the well-kept potato rows. The hermit looked soberly at me and stopped to shake my hand. 'He'll grow up to tell a great story,' I remember him saying, but I was tongue-tied and said nothing. In Paddy's world the telling of a story was a most important skill. He set great store by stories and in this he was encouraged by Grandfather who considered himself no mean teller of tales. Grandfather propped himself on the drystone wall Paddy had built to protect and shelter his crop and I found a stone on which to sit, which wasn't difficult. The stones outnumbered anything else and it was said that Paddy planted his potatoes under them and they grew in the meagre compost beneath. The sun warmed the stones and the potatoes came early. There was hardly any need to cultivate or hoe for there wasn't enough soil for both potatoes and weeds. I didn't notice, of course, for I was too young to appreciate such points, but long afterwards remembered it when people talked about the fine potatoes to be had on the west coast of Scotland where farmers didn't plough but set their seed among the stones.

After he had finished his task Paddy led us out of the garden and along to his cave. The pigeons flew out as we went in. A lean black cat with green, slit eyes whipped past us as we entered and went off up the rocks to wait until we departed again. Paddy said she just didn't like people. She too was a recluse. Robinson Crusoe or the Swiss Family

Robinson would have approved of Paddy's cave. He had made it comfortable by rescuing things from the shore after the winter gales. He had two presentable leather armchairs, the springs of which had probably rusted in the salt water but appeared none the worse for that. He had a heavy table that had been bundled and bashed against the rocks more than a little before he found it but stood solid and square where he had planted it in the debris of the floor of the cave. He had several lanterns and every kind of pot and pan hung on the wall. The sea had given up everything he needed while it had undoubtedly taken the owners of some of the items. I remember touching a 'squeeze-box' that wailed as I disturbed it, and Paddy shaking his head and saying the poor sailor who had owned it had gone aloft like Tom Bowling, for that day everything a boat could carry and could float had come bobbing and washing in the shallows along with the clothing of the crew whose rescue was never achieved. There was a notched stick out by the door, some kind of log marker I suppose it was, but a cousin who came back to the trap with it at the end of our picnic saw it as something more sinister – the notches had been made on the stick by the villainous captain of the foundered vessel, one for each member of the crew he had killed on the voyage! I couldn't make up my mind about this but the flotsam of the shore Paddy had rescued included a blackened picture frame displaying a sort of photogravure image of a buxom woman who had been, Paddy suggested, the captain's good lady or perhaps his mother. The frame was silver, he said, but alas no metal polish had been washed up and it had never been cleaned. The round-faced, stern lady looked at us from a ledge on which Paddy kept a tea caddy, a candle stick and a spyglass. Sometimes he would spend a whole morning looking westwards at the coast of Ireland. Away out there, across the whole green island, on the far shore where the Atlantic rolled in, he had spent his boyhood 'with the geese coming down along the coast in Autumn and the turf fires burning without ever going out.'

The Idler's Companion

Angus

ONCE, THERE WAS NO DOUBT, he had looked a very fine figure of a young man in the uniform of an officer. Once he had climbed the parapet with a revolver in his hand and a whistle in his mouth, to urge the infantryman with a fixed bayonet to his work. The rush of air-rending shells and the odour of burning cordite had taken the country boy's colour from his cheeks and he had little to remind him of the bright visions of glory he had before this trauma had befallen him. He still had, however, an inborn self-respect that made him polish his brown boots, wear a carefully tied tie, a clean shirt, a waistcoat with fancy buttons, a handkerchief in his breast pocket. He brushed his thinning hair and kept his moustache trimmed in military fashion. The world to which he returned, having no exact category in which to put him, dubbed him a gentleman, which he was and always had been. He addressed his elders with respect. My aunts were accorded their proper title of miss. Even a small boy was 'master'. To be respected one must show respect and must have respect. This was Angus's creed. There were some who said he was a bit of an old woman, but invariably these were men who didn't know where Angus had been, or what it was like on the Somme where he had been tested in the fire. A man who read teacups must be a kind of Jesse, they said. They didn't say it to him. If they had I think he would have bowed slightly and smiled a sad smile. He had been under more frightening fire.

The Idler's Companion

Sojer Scott

THE OLD MAN TOLD THE pony to steady up and we trundled past the Sojer in his greatcoat. At a distance of about six paces Sojer Scott jerked his arm up to salute and held that position until we were past him. He brought his arm down again and remained standing there for as long as I could look back at him, but I have no doubt that once we were out of sight he resumed his slow progress along the road. He travelled at a snail's pace, I discovered. He was still on that stretch of quiet road when we returned and once again the pony was slowed (in case he shied at the sudden throwing up of the Sojer's arm) and we went steadily past without acknowledging his salute.

'God knows what's in the mind of him.' Grandfather said, 'but it pleases him to do that. If you speak to him he won't answer but when you're passed his poor mind will boil over and he'll get up to all kinds of military antics, stepping back and stepping forward, turning this way and that, and marching away with his arms swinging. The war scrambled his wits I've no doubt.'

The Idler's Companion

The Blacksmith

THE BLACKSMITH, WHO COULD hardly keep his tools in his hands on certain days when the trout were in the pool below the bridge, often went angling. When he deserted the smithy he would leave a note on the door for any farmer who called. It would state briefly, 'Up the water' or 'Down the water', and the caller would either go away or go up or down the water to find the smith. I remember calling with a mare that needed a set of shoes, and at the moment of my arrival the smith was padlocking his door. I tied the mare to a ring in the wall and went with him. He was going fishing, he informed me. He had a hammer in his hand and I could see no sign of a rod, or even a piece of brown line. I followed him a yard or two to the bank, where he sat down and took off his boots and socks and turned up the bottom of his trousers. 'Come on,' he said. 'You might as well. The mare'll not be shod till I've done.' He had stopped the water with a dam, he told me, and now he was going fishing with a big hammer. Obediently, for I could be persuaded to any such pastime with a glance of invitation, I took off my boots and socks and waded into the stream after the smith, gasping at the coldness of the water and making grimaces of pain as I trod on a stone not so smooth as it might have been. We came to the first pool. The smith signalled to me and I stood down water from him as he indicated. He swung the heavy hammer above his head. The sinews of his wrists rose and the hammer came down with a great crash on the nearest rock. I caught my breath, for a moment later a stunned fish floated out.

'Grab it!' yelled the smith.

I grabbed and managed to get it. We waded a few paces

and he struck another rock but no trout had sheltered beneath. We moved again and he struck another without result. All at once he stopped.

'Hell,' he said, 'look yonder!'

His landlord, carrying basket and rod, was coming up the bank. We scampered to our boots. The smith lifted his and ran over the cinders to unlock the smithy door. With the fish in my pocket, and my boots untied on my feet, I hurried after him and led the mare in to be shod. He had put on his boots and was pulling at the handle of the bellows.

'If he shows face in the door,' he cursed, 'I'll put a hot iron on him.'

The owner of the smithy and the stream went past and the mare was shod. I promised myself I would get down to 'fish' with the smith again, but somehow the opportunity never arose.

The Poacher's Handbook

Jack Bopeep

HE WAS A THIN, PINCH-FACED little man, who looked to me as though he had once suffered from jaundice, and when I met him on the road out of the village on that first occasion I took him for a shepherd in spite of his sallow complexion. I must admit that it was the crook that did it. He held it in the right way. A crook in the hands of a mere hiker or walker, for instance, would look like a too-long walking stick and a cumbersome thing. The way the little man carried it I knew he was a flockmaster. He nodded to me. I guessed he was in a hurry to attend a lambing ewe, for it was early spring, and the little Welsh ewes were busy having lambs which they would later take with them to the mountain slopes. I saw my 'shepherd' several times after that and we exchanged greetings. Once he was leaning over a gate gazing at some sheep being gathered by a dog along a fence at the top end of the field.

'Steady now!' he said almost under his breath, and I guessed he had sent the dog to do something with the sheep, but all it did was bunch them and then come trotting all the way to the gate, and I wondered why it had driven them up there.

'They're in shelter up there, see?' the little man said, and turned and went plodding down the road. The dog slunk at his heel as though tied to him by a cord. The crook half trailed on the ground. The little man impressed me as a busy fellow with little time to stand and gossip, but then keeping sheep is hard work. Spring, summer, or winter there is a lot to be done with them. Between whiles they have to be taken to market.

I was having a drink in the pub when I saw my man again and he nodded to me, and I felt I should offer him a pint.

'The gentleman over there,' I told the barman, 'the shepherd.'

The barman grinned at me. 'Jack Bopeep,' he said.

… It was some time before I discovered that Jack wasn't a shepherd in the proper sense of the word. He didn't rent any grazing. He lived in the village. He had a Welsh collie that went everywhere with him, but he worked for the council! All at once I began to see him as a character in his own right. Jack never lost his sheep. He spent his time looking for them, and everyone, except an incomer like myself, knew about him.

. . . When I came to study him I smiled to think that I

could ever have mistaken him for a shepherd. If there is one thing a shepherd is not, it is restless and in a hurry. A shepherd is a phlegmatic, plodding man, who knows he will never last out if he runs or rushes. He covers so many miles in a day he must pace himself. It is in the nature of sheep to move at walking pace and no more. Rush them and they run up banks, pour over walls, break through hedges and get tangled in blackberry bushes and thorns. Jack Bopeep, I concluded was a poseur. He wanted gullible people like myself to mistake him for the owner of a great flock of sheep, a man of substance who attended ram sales, and never missed a market held every Monday in the town five miles away. For a while this explanation satisfied me. I smiled when I passed Jack Bopeep in the street, imagining that he put on his act for me, and passed me marching to attention. It was one of the reasons why our exchanges were confined to the weather. He didn't want to tell me more. Any conclusion I came to would be my own. Jack Bopeep would hurry on, without being in the least inhibited by any story he might have planted in my mind! If I took him for a shepherd that would be my lookout. People would laugh at me. They knew him. There has to be an end to conjecture and speculation of this kind, and it was left to me to ask people. I didn't ask, and I began to revise my ideas when I actually saw Jack with his crook about the neck of a sheep which he was bringing down the road with his dog keeping the animal forging on while the crook acted as a restraint. So, I said, he keeps sheep in his spare time, at least one sheep, for he took the sheep all the way down the road to the house where he lived at the tail end of the village, and bundled it through the front gate, up the path and right into the house! The door closed upon all three of them, and that was that. Jack Bopeep didn't always lose his sheep! Sometimes he found them, and, it seems, brought them home to supper. The sheep, of course, without my knowing it had been bundled straight on through the house into the back garden. This was something Jack did once in a while.

The Idler's Companion

Boy in the Beanfield

IN SOUND OF THE WAVES washing up the sand, the boy worked in the beanfield. The beans were as tall as the crown of his head. He just walked among them, picking until his sack was full, but he walked carefully so that nothing was missed and he never lost himself in that forest of swaying stalks.

Such a picture he gave me of a day in his boyhood. He told me too, of the 'tippeny school'. For twopence a week, until he or his father called enough, they taught him to read and write and count. The world taught him the rest; that there was money for bundling carrots in dozens, and if he played scarecrow, pigeons at harvest time were worth two-pence a pair.

When it came to shooting pigeons the world taught him his first real lesson. Given a blunderbuss, a pouch of lead, a pouch of powder and a powder-horn, he perched in a tree to shoot pigeons feeding on a field of ripening oats. The roar of the gun and the falling birds scared the pigeons on to the adjoining field of oats, owned by another farmer. As the day went on the farmer paid him a visit. His powder would be supplied free, and pigeons would be threepence a pair if he shot to the left instead of to the right. He changed employers there and then, but remained sitting in the same tree. Before sunset pigeons were fivepence a pair, lead and powder was free, and he had to think before he fired, left or right? His employer was the man who had last raised the price a halfpenny and so increased the value of his string of battered and blood bespattered birds.

It taught him the law of demand. When the harvesting was drawing to a close and the carts were rolling away the last few sheaves, instead of offering him powder and lead they were telling him to 'Git tae hell oot o' that tree, or I'll ha' the law on ye for poachin'. In the end there was no money left for powder and lead. He used his last loading in a thunderous shot in the air which brought a branch down on his head, knocking him to the ground. The day's bag was disposed of after argument and bargaining at cottager's doors in the gloaming, when, as he said, the cold air had set in and the howlerts were flapping across the fields.

However, such a life was not good enough for a lad, decided his father, son of a failed farmer. The land was a hard life. The railway was coming into the country. They had cut its path through the rocks of Kirkcudbright and the spluttering contraption of an engine was scaring horses at ploughing and harvest and leaving simple folk staring with mouths agape. They would make him a railway man. Accordingly a letter was written, and after a week or so, dressed in a new suit of clothes, with his shirt and socks in a bundle, he went off across the county to 'learn to be a porter' at a station where the train, the only train, called twice a day, to pick up a basket of eggs or unload a bag of artificial manure. He and the stationmaster lived together, but only for a day or two. One morning the train unhitched a wagon of coal to be unloaded. The wagon stood a foot or so from the end of the platform. The stationmaster stepped down and fiddled with the brake, his foot slipped on a wet rail, and the wagon, unbraked on a slight slope, trundled forward and took his leg off at the thigh.

By the time help arrived the stationmaster was dead. It was enough. The following morning the train carried away, in addition to the basket of eggs, the acting stationmaster and the apprentice porter. The station was left deserted. Sometime in the afternoon he arrived home. His mother was at the girdle, her arms flour-dusty to the elbows. She belted him until his dark suit was as floury as her arms had been. Here he was, a growing man, deserting his work and leaving the railway without help. He was a disgrace. His father's thoughts were much the same, and the railway company seemed to resent the desertion too, for they sent word the following morning that they expected him back at the station the next day. He made the journey and was told at the end of it that the company had washed its hands of him and his wages would pay his fare home.

It was grand fun, he told me, riding back and forward across the county, seeing horses tossing their heads and prancing as they passed; seeing whole families standing at cottage doors staring at the engine; jogging and swaying round the sides of green hills and dizzily crossing bridges over lonely streams. He returned with the distinction of being the most travelled person in the village. Men who made a similar journey sought him out when telling their friends so that they might agree that it took half-an-hour from such a place to so and so.

My Childhood

*I can remember quite clearly now a recuperating soldier singing to
me Gaelic songs but I can also remember small, insignificant
things – the sound of a porridge pot bubbling; talk on a wet
Sunday when the hills were veiled in mist; the clatter and laughter of dancers on the tiled floor of the kitchen when the vigour of
their gyrations set up a draught that made the oil-lamp smoke.*
My Childhood

3
Tall Trees and Bright Mornings

I WASN'T BORN IN GALLOWAY, which comprises Wigtownshire and the Stewarty of Kirkcudbright, nor yet in Kyle, but further north. My father was born in Galloway and his family had been there as long as there had been parish records, and even longer. It didn't do to whisper that they might have originated anywhere else, a great-aunt or –uncle having come across the water from Ireland, and indeed no one did. With the passing of more than half my years I understand the colourful imagination they had, the gift for turning a phrase and if it wasn't exactly Irish it was certain Gaelic in descriptiveness.

'The morn's morn,' my grandfather would say to one of his men, 'you'll take old Bob and go up to the moss and cut a wheen of peats against the winter's cold.' And in the morning the man would go to the peat moss and cut some peats to be aired and dried and finally brought home to give us a winter fire so hot, so aromatic and so oxygen-consuming, that the entire family would fall asleep in their chairs after supper and only awake when the wick of the oil lamp had burned low and the grey ash of the peats had finally fallen through the bars of the grate.

A Galloway Childhood

Coming out of the high planting one stood on the crown of Clutag's highest hill, looking down over undulating country,

the twisting road, the march gate, the thick little wood sur-
rounding the schoolhouse and the smithy and the winding
water of the river. In the hollow there, Clutag's steading, the
stackyard, the back piggery and the stable midden; the farm-
house with its assortment of chimneys, the square white-
washed stacks, the red, yellow and cream chimney pots.
My Childhood

When the sun shone in the brilliance of spring I loved to
breathe the intoxicating air that the breeze carried from the
far moss. I firmly believed that there was nothing in the
whole world going beyond our march wall to see. Here I
could gaze upon blue hills to the north and all the patch-
work of pasture and ploughing in between the winding glint
of the river and fir plantings along lesser hills.
My Childhood

I travelled on my grandmother's back to see the chickens
fed; I was carried to see the pig mash and the cows brought
in. It was always time for something or other. The hours
chimed and one rose to take a tea basket to the switchback
hill or the wee five-acre and another hastened to the
Hillhead for the letters and yesterday's daily newspaper.
My Childhood

The Wee Field was my playground. It had everything a child
could desire, round hillocks of gorse, gentle slopes, a drystone wall. A thorn hedge, a burn with peaty banks, places
where laying-away hens nested, waterholes where the ducks
left their eggs. Here the wagtail pinned his nest above the

burn and here were the holes of the water vole. In this place I watched the breeze make a speeding ship of a curling white feather, and here too I toppled into the mud and came out like a black man, yelling for my mother. When I discovered the secrets of setting a snare, it was here I set my first, watched by my grandmother. Grandmother believed in encouraging a child in its play. She went to the harvest field where a rabbit had been killed by the binder, brought back the carcass and put it in my snare. I was not to be deceived, however. I knew my rabbit had been killed by the binder knife. No amount of praise made me satisfied that I had caught my dinner. I was born country-wise.

Pastures New

Because I was without the company of other children when I was very small I had to amuse myself to a great extent. I was a little venturesome – once the flooded midden almost swallowed me to the ears – more than once I fell in the burn, but most of the time I played games that aped my elders, walking with a bit of a stick and counting imaginary sheep and carrying an old sawn-down muzzle-loading gun. I carried the old gun because grandfather allowed me to follow him at a great distance when he went round the field in search of something for the pot, usually a pheasant he had marked as it picked its way through the whins. When I was not playing one of my games I liked to search the peat dust where the hens fluffed their feathers, for here I often found bits of brightly-patterned china. Now that I think of it I can almost see them being hidden there after some accident with one of grandmother's best teasets.

My Childhood

The low planting was a forbidden place. I could go anywhere but there. Once or twice a year a pole-barred entrance was cleared and grandfather and one of his men went to cut 'stobs' or stack props, but as soon as this work was done the wood was closed and no foot as much as cracked a stick within its boundary. I think the first thing that lured me in was a red squirrel swinging and throwing itself from one treetop to the next, and after that, a mossy nest with white feathers protruding from its dainty opening, and then the cry of a bird, a black rabbit, the rooks, a hare, the magic of the place itself, the very talk of the wind through the roof of dark green conifer branches. Here, with the bracken a sea about me, I could stand and stare at the small bird searching the bark for insects, or play a game of hide-and-seek with a squirrel that imagined itself concealed on the far side of a bough. I began to go into the wood regularly, and thought it as well to go in on my hands and knees over a bit of bare ground, like the collie, so that my place of entry would not be advertised by broken and crushed grass and obvious footprints.

Perhaps I returned from the direction so often the household came to know that I was breaking a commandment, for they began to call me from the wood regularly. I would be standing there, admiring some bright fungi, or testing my nose by locating the stinkhorn without looking, or just daydreaming, and I would hear that faint call across the hollow. The calling distracted me for a moment, but no longer than the sound of a bee in the foxglove, the call of the curlew crossing from one stretch of moor to another. How well my doting aunts knew me. Their summons was always without confidence. They would come out to the steading fence, look towards the low planting and call my name. More often than not their arms were dusty with flour from the baking board. They had something special cooking in the oven or on the girdle and had to hurry back to save it and they sighed as they went back indoors, saying. 'That boy will meet his death away there in the planting.'

Of course, they did not believe what they said. When I returned, they picked the long gorse thorns from my jersey, or the seat of my trousers, looked at my water-logged boots, at my bog-blackened feet and shook their heads ruefully, promising that my parents would be told; that it was more than flesh and blood could stand, and I must go back to the town where policemen kept small boys in order.

My Childhood

To be treated by grandfather was to be handled firmly. He would not tolerate wriggling or whimpering and his treatment was generally beneficial.

I had been playing in the stackyard at threshing time and a day later I found I had a pain in my ear. The pain became so bad I could hardly bear it. My ear quickly became inflamed and one of my aunts noticed that I wasn't myself. She told grandfather and he called me. I stood between his legs and he looked at my ear. The moment he touched me I felt a stab of pain so terrible that I sprang from him and raced through the door. Grandfather stamped after me. My aunts began to run, grandmother called in the background. I raced up the old road, barefooted and terrified. The family ran after me. A spectator would have had a laugh as past the cartshed we ran in a straggling line, and up the road beside the stacks. They were relentless in pursuit. Determined to catch me and see what gave me pain. I began to lose breath. They drew near and I stopped and put my finger into my ear and extracted a short, sharp piece of straw that had been cutting into my tender flesh. The family descended upon me and smiling and crying at once, I displayed the fragment of straw.

'That was a carry-on,' said grandfather as he examined the ear. 'I have a good mind to bump your backside . . . '
My Childhood

Well if it didn't happen I heard it told with a wonderful resemblance to the truth. I was small and the atmosphere of the kitchen with its salt ham hanging from the ceiling, the cats snoozing in the hearth and the iron kettle singing on the big, burnished range, was as heady to me as the malting-floor of the distillery and the fume of the spirits was to some of my kin.

'Boy, d'ye ken what I'm going to tell ye?' one would begin. My eyes would grow large with wonder and I would listen to stories of the world not as it was, or had been, with everything in sharp contrast, comedy and tragedy, joy and despair. Now and again someone would shake his head and remark on the things I was learning about people and the world. I would grow up old-fashioned, they would swear, and my head would be full of nonsense, which was probably true. To counteract this, my Grandfather would read to me from The Scottish Farmer. There was nothing like a bit of news on the latest method of treating footrot in black-faced sheep to adjust my tendency to attach too much importance to old men's tales.
A Galloway Childhood

Wet days in plenty troubled those who had work to do, but they didn't trouble a child overmuch when he could watch the ducks leaving the gig house and taking a shower where the corrugated iron of the shed poured a deluge on the stony ground beneath. They loved the rain for they belonged to the wet and their delight was a laughable contrast to the dejection and misery of almost every other creature, the horse with his rear end turned towards the rain, the wet and bedraggled fowls that roosted in spars and preened their 'drook-ed' feathers and looked like bundles of wet rag. Out to the burn went the ducks without anyone to say nay, and out to the burn I would go too, if I could slip away to sail a boat or wade the spate and watch the ducks swim on under the road and into the tunnels of over-hanging grass and dripping hawthorns and broom bushes.

'It's a wet one,' someone would say, stamping his feet to shake rain from his clothes and batting his old tweed cap against the lime-washed wall of the stable, cursing the weather that delayed hay-making or some urgent duty. The heron fished in the rain and along the shelter of the hedge-side the hare loped and grazed and peewits flew from one water-logged field to the next. Out of the mist came the cormorants crossing land between bays and swimming in the air almost as easily and gracefully as they did in deep water after fish.

When I discovered how to fish and learned that spate brought out the biggest trout to feed, I came to love the rain. I would deck myself in oilskin coat and hat and take myself off to fish in the burn fed ... on into the magic world of gliding water and trailing weed and inundated round rushes where rain sizzled down and crept along stalks and pattered on the riverside waterlillies. Over my boot-heads I would go, they said, and come home with wet feet and that was bad enough, but I might find myself in deeper water and sail away to the sea with the ricks that the flood picked up in the water-meadows and dead old trees and gates and barrels and chicken coops. They were often angry with me for the fright I gave them when I managed to slip away in the rain. Was it not enough that clothes had to be dried for men who had been drenched at work, not enough that ducks and ducklings had to be shepherded back and the floor of the kitchen washed a score of times to remove the pattern of mud and wet boots? The dogs stayed at home in the rain. Rain was for the wild duck and the scarts and herons.

A Galloway Childhood

Fear of grandfather's displeasure produced strange results. I remember helping him to bring down a ram from the hill. The ram was a very agile creature and had broken through to other farms so often that it had been decided to sacrifice him for the butcher's cheque. We locked the ram in the strawhouse and grandfather himself set out for the town to bring back the butcher and his implements, for part of his bargain included a joint of mutton to be retained at Clutag. The trap had hardly left the steading when I was tempted to look at the ram. To my dismay he charged past me, raced through an open gate and made off for the hills. What could I do? In an hour or so the butcher would arrive. I had to get the ram back without anyone knowing. Before he was across the field I began to run after him. I ran across boggy ground, through thistles and blackberry tangle. I ran until my lungs seemed inflamed. I was weak and in tears, and the ram remained a few yards ahead of me. He bounded over a wall,

I stumbled and clambered after him. He splashed through the stream. We crossed acres of clover and my feet pained me as I ran through stones, for I had discarded my shoes in order to run the faster. The ram was strong. He had sinews like the thong of the binder whip, but it was hot. He began to take intervals of resting, halting for a second and panting before going on and I began to gain ground. At length I threw myself upon him, burying my frantic hands in his thick wool. I fell and grabbed one of his horns. Now I had him. I knew how to move him to the drystone wall where I found a piece of grass rope and secured him with a hobble. In half an hour I had him back in the strawhouse. He seemed glad to stand there in the darkness, getting his wind and wondering what madness had induced him to break away.

Later in the afternoon the butcher arrived and in due course came to do his gory work in the strawhouse. He caught the ram's horn and turned him so he could examine his condition.

'Do you know,' he said to grandfather, 'you'd think this one was broken winded, just like an old horse!'

My Childhood

Everyone about Clutag came in for certain duties. Mine included feeding calves and it was a job that required strength at times, for the calves had a habit of tossing pails when they had licked them round and sometimes they butted into them with their hard little heads, driving the rims against my shins. Another duty was that of egg gathering. This was a pleasure, because it entailed searching for the nests of the hens that laid away. The search took me through the dock weeds in the old stackyard, the nettles that screened the broken plough, through all the dark corners in the barn, the chaff house, the stable, the back piggery and the front pighouses. I was not always too particular whether I found the nest or not. I had the thrill of coming on the litter of kittens, disturbing a rat, finding the nest of a robin in an old can or discovering the duck's nest in the gorse clump. How the old duck hissed and snapped as she sat tightly along the dead grass and fine down.

Of course there were tasks much less to my liking. I had to feed the turnip cutter or stir mash and one autumn I had to do my bit in the potato field. The work in the potato field was exciting for the first hour. I loved to see the black earth being thrown up by the digger and the red and purple potatoes falling on the freshly disturbed soil. We gathered the potatoes in cans. In a little while everybody began to feel the strain. It was back-aching work, and one potato was no different from another. I did my share for about an hour and then began to feel hungry and exhausted. What could I do? There was no escape. Grandfather circled the field with the digger. Nothing missed his eye. He even marked the spot where the covey of partridges settled when they took off from beneath his horses' feet. I could think of no way to escape until I decided to get into one of the cans and roll myself slowly out of the field. I did not think a rolling can would be noticed. I was so hungry and tired and in the kitchen they were baking, for it was about half-past two. The journey in the rolling can was most uncomfortable. Once I rolled out, but quickly crawled back in again. The can was on the hard ground by the gate when I felt safe. I got to my feet and began to walk quickly away when I heard the laughter of those who had been working. They had stood watching the rolling pail from which the lower half of my body had protruded. I took off for home as fast as I could go, leaving everyone in fits of laughter.

'Did you get tired, boy?' asked grandfather at supper time. I looked angrily at the ploughman who was grinning.

'No,' I said, 'I wasn't tired. I was just going home for a scone.'

My Childhood

In one of the bright dry intervals between turnip thinning and hay harvest it would be decided that it was time some peats were cut. The peat moss was away in the west, up a winding stony road bounded by ferny banks that were the home of countless rabbits. So infrequent was the traffic on this road that the stones in the centre were broken by shoots of fine green grass. Indeed, most of the day on the moss road was quiet; the small bird sang on the stunted thorn, an adder rustled the dry turf and now and then a black grouse rose and cackled. To anticipate a day at the peat was almost unbearable, but more often than not peat cutting was decided upon at breakfast, a basket packed with things for lunch and a horse yoked to the cart before the sun had really got his glow beyond the shoulder of the big hill. Down the farm road the cart jolted and jerked through potholes, making the peat cutters slide and clatter, but once on the high road, or, as the old-fashioned and older people called it, the King's road, progress was steady and comfortable. I preferred to sit watching the road appearing from beneath the tail of the cart. By doing this I deprived myself of the sight of the sun across it broken only by the shadow of a speeding cloud. I liked to close my eyes and listen to the change in the sound of the cartwheels as we passed under the ash trees near the signpost and the road junction, but most of all I liked to stare at the people who came out of their cottages to stare unashamedly at our passing.

The piece of moss my grandfather rented was in a hollow. It has been used for years and the peats were in terraces. In very wet weather the lower part flooded. No one knew how deep the moss was. The primeval forests that had made it must have lasted an age, for in the dry weather it was impossible to cut below the peat. Now and then the cutters might find what we called a moss-block and an effort was always made to dig it out for winter fires. These blocks were really ancient trees, perhaps oak, that had sunk into the decaying forest and become almost petrified. As hard as stone, they were. After a saw had been used on a moss-block it was useless for anything else and my grandfather always swore that there was a second heat in them, the first being the heat engendered trying to cut them to a suitable size for burning.

This day at the moss was one of the great events of each summer. To eat out in the wild waste, among the heather and the cotton grass, to get my feet wet in the moss-bottomed waterholes and have my heart beat fast at the sight of an adder. I took a fascinated interest in adders. Grandfather never ceased to warn me to keep away from the stone piles and watch out for adders, particularly the little black adder or the one that had a reddish appearance. Once I found an adder I was so frightened I gave the spot a wide berth, but invariably I had to look for one. The day at the moss lacked something unless I could recall the hissing glide of the snake as it vanished among the twisted roots on some heather bank. There were other things that made that day. They were to see someone passing along the distant road and to wonder who they were and where they were going, to be startled by the sudden rising of a flock of grouse or find the disused nest of a curlew or peewit, no more than a rounded hollow on some tufted mound, and, finally to go back through the wood, see the lodge, the rabbits impudently sporting themselves on the road and the smoke rising from the cottages behind the hillocks round which the road wound.

The peats were brought home with two carts and unloaded as gently as possible. On the following day grandfather and one of his men would stack them. Sometimes they were made into a peat stack, a solid block of peats not unlike a cottage. Over the roof of the cottage was arranged a thatch and the peats were carefully taken from the building in baskets each day throughout the year so that the remainder was always dry and tidy. Sometimes, however, it was more convenient to stack them in a shed and in this event they were carried in wire turnip baskets and built solidly into the shed, right to the roof. It was, of course, impossible to fill the last few inches, and this gap was always the spot chosen by the laying-away hen or the cat that raised a wild brood of kittens.

My Childhood

When I was a small boy, if people didn't get down on their knees and pray for a good harvest, for the rain to hold off and the crop to be brought safely in, it was because they worked hard and work was a prayer in itself.

A Galloway Childhood

I used to get under their feet when the time came to haul the binder out of the black shed where it had stood brooding for ten months of the year. Getting the binder out meant that we were almost on the brink of the greatest effort of the year, a more protracted effort than the steam-mill threshing-day, as urgent as hay-making, but a far, far bigger task. The binder's joints were likely to be stiff and creaky. It had been a perching-place for the more venturesome fowls. It was bogged down in the litter on the floor, the residue of peats stacked in the big tarred shed, the litter of straw and hurriedly stored hay. It trundled out of the court, a squealing, rattling monster with its working parts in need of cleaning because of those roosting chickens, its scored-away sheets needing draining or patching, its cogs greasing, its chains turning and its levers, for lowering the knife bar, checking over. It often seemed that it would never be itself again and would never perform its urgent task, rock and sway and hurry round the rapidly diminishing field, with its great wheel getting polished and shining, rolling over miles of stubbles and countless boulders.

A Galloway Childhood

In the fields the corn was ripening from a pale green to a pale gold – acres of oats and barley and sometimes rye. Oats, however, were the important crop. We had more oats than anything else, oat-straw to bed the standing-in cows in winter, and to make the horses comfortable in the stable, grain to be bruised and fed to the stock mash, taken to the mill and made into oatmeal for our porridge, or exchanged for white flour. The whole economy depended on the milking-cow, and the cow depended on the corn. The gathering in of corn was a challenge that every member of the family had to face. We were all harvesters. While no one knew the date on which the harvest would begin, for corn ripened the way the first swallow came on the ridge of the barn or the geese came south in October, there were certain arrangements that had to be made in preparation for that day. We had to be sure that we had all the help we could muster. We had to 'wage' harvesters and everyone else in the countryside was concerned to do the same. We could get an odd man here or there who would promise 'a day', but it was necessary to be more sure of help than any casual promise. Grandfather would 'write away' for harvesters. An agent across the water in Ireland would arrange contracts with small farmers prepared to come over and work in the corn-fields of Galloway and other parts of south-west Scotland. It was an ancient custom, this hiring of harvesters.

A Galloway Childhood

Rain produced frustration but lying corn was an annual bugbear. When this happened the corn had to be lifted with a rake handle and set against the knives of the machine so that it could be cut without waste or the machine bogging down. Worst of all, however, was the crisis that came when the binder broke down and some vital part was found to have fractured or worn away. This kind of crisis could come at any time but it hardly ever occurred when the last half acre was being cut. Nor did it happen early on, but nearly always in the middle of a task, on a clear bright day when everything was going well, when the horses were thudding along, the tall corn was rippling over the knives and tumbling under the flail and everyone was in high spirits, the birds singing in the tree and the sun blazing down upon us. Such a sudden coming to a halt was unreal. The silence itself was unnatural. It was never long before everyone was out of the rhythm of the work and most of the harvesters were sitting on fallen sheaves, searching their shirts for seeds that tickled their skin, or drawing on stumps of cigarettes hastily put into pockets at the onset of the afternoon's labour.

While the horses dipped their heads to snatch mouthfuls of growing corn, tearing it up by the roots, Grandfather would be on his hands and knees studying the machine to see what had caused it to come to a standstill. It didn't take him long to find the cause but it sometimes took a while to decide on the best course of action. He would pull out his watch and look about him. He knew who had an old binder of the same model and mark. He wondered if it had a spare part, and how long it would take to replace the broken piece. He decided whether the horses would be taken away, fed and watered and put out to graze, yoked to the reaper, or kept in the field while the spare part was obtained. No neighbour who could oblige in such circumstances would dream of refusing help. Sometimes the broken part could be mended at the smithy and Grandfather would hurry off down there to make a repair so that no more than an hour or two would be lost. Sometimes the reaper was the only way unless another binder could be borrowed. The harvesters were impatient to get on. They knew a harvest day to be the precious thing it was, a God-sent day when it was man's duty to toil and reap the field as quickly as he could.

A Galloway Childhood

Many a farm child had met with an accident in the corn-field. Grandfather solved this problem in a practical fashion by fitting another seat on the binder. I sailed round with him while the corn was cut, well out of the way of the great feet of the Clydesdales or the running knives that brought corn to the canvas. I never was afraid of horses after that, except perhaps, ponies. I loved the draught horse, the magnificent beast that thrust his great shoulders into the collar and struck the soft earth with his hindfeet as he pounded uphill, making the binder shake and vibrate, disgorging a sheaf every few seconds.

A Galloway Childhood

. . . one or other of the women folk would begin to blow life into the fire, breaking off now and then to go to the foot of 'the men's stair' and make an effort to rouse the byreman and the ploughman.

My Childhood

In order that the milk might reach the creamery in reasonable time, the cows had to be brought in in summer and milked as quickly as possible, for the churns had to be cooled in great tubs of water in order that the milk might arrive fresh at the creamery. Farmers who were in too much of a hurry had often to bring their milk back and pour it in the piggery troughs. At Clutag such waste was avoided. The milking took place early. Once the churns were cool they were loaded on the spring cart and the pony took off down the rough road. At the road end he was urged into a trot and the milk went into the creamery vats somewhere between nine and ten o-clock.

Before the milking was half finished, I would be sum-
moned from bed. How crisp were those mornings. How
often the court was frozen and hoar frost covered the currant
bush by the door. It was not a law that I went to the creamery. Had I wished, I could have stayed in bed, but the creamery ride was an adventure. Down in the kitchen I would have
found my breakfast on the bars of the range oven, a plate
covered by a bowl, beneath the bowl, fried potato scone, salt
bacon, egg. At my place at table would be a bowl of cream
and a bowl into which I might ladle my porridge. At that
busy hour of the morning no one had time to stay waiting at
table. The family came down or came in and each identified
his breakfast in the oven. The men did the same. Their breakfast plates were usually ranged along the rack above the fire.
The plates were always so hot that one had to hurry to the
table before the heat penetrated through the tea cloth. This
was all part of the creamery ride for me; this sitting in the
kitchen, half-awake, staring at the dawn coming up behind
the eastern hills, listening to the newly kindled fire roaring in
the chimney, feeling snug and at home in the turned-down
glimmer of the oil-lamp. In an hour someone would come
clattering across to the house, blowing his nails or flailing his
arms against his ribs. The morning conversation was poor,
but in the morning I was always contemplative. For a long
time my life seemed to be mornings. After noon the day lost
its magic. The progress of the sun seemed slower, less magnificent after noon. Only at evening did beauty return and
something of the mystic power gather; then the gloaming
shadows stirred the imagination; things had magic again, like
the swinging progress of a storm lantern carried round the
out-buildings on a locking-up tour, or the bars of light from
between the slats of the stable shutters.

'You're off to the creamery?' the byreman would ask.

Off to the creamery; part of the coming to life of a quiet countryside, the gritting of wheels on the hard roads, the clop and clatter of the hooves of horses, the far-away singing of some light-hearted driver perched among his churns. It was necessary to wrap up like an arctic explorer. I was never mollycoddled. Red cheeks were considered a sign of health, but on the creamery ride the family were at pains to see that I was warm. I often had my head wrapped in a scarf and wore a cap perched on top. I wore gloves and sometimes mittens as well. I wore my top-coat and something to wrap round my knees if necessary, for the coldest place to ride is on the fore-end of a spring cart on a bitter morning.

The milk had to be taken some five miles to the creamery. Most of the farmers conveyed it themselves. The charge for having it collected made too large an inroad in the meagre profit. I think the haulier lifted churns at road-ends for something like a farthing a gallon, and a farthing a gallon was considerable when the price of milk was so low.

My Childhood

Like the men, Grandfather found something disturbing in the mere thought of idleness. He was probably a slave-driver. Most farmers at that time had to drive hard to make ends meet. He would come to the stable to see if he could find some sort of work to occupy his men. The chaff house might be emptied, the cartshed tidied, the calf house cleaned, the barn floor scraped, pigs re-bedded, harness sorted, sacks repaired. Once in a while he set the men to making a variety of ropes with a rope weaving device he had invented, a piece of equipment that made use of lengths of binder twine to make plough lines, ropes for tarpaulin sheets and draught ropes. It was a business that required supervision and took a considerable amount of time, in consequence of which it was never embarked upon unless the weather had been carefully checked. It was no use beginning to make a rope and then abandoning the project when the sun came out and in any case a damp atmosphere was essential for the weaving of the sisal. I was fascinated to see them making ropes which they did on the byre walk, the only building with the length necessary for the purpose. Sometimes I had visions of even longer ropes being made by the same process in great long buildings covering miles of bricked floor. I was disappointed to learn that machines did the job faster, although not any better.

A Galloway Childhood

How enthusiastically we lived, how cold it was on those winter mornings when the pump had to be thawed with a great kettle of boiling water, and how peaceful it was on Sunday, when they went off to the kirk with the pony specially groomed, the harness polished, the brass and gig lamps burnished and Grandmother and Grandfather 'decked off' in their Sunday clothes.

A Galloway Childhood

Singing on Sunday was hymn singing. No cards were played. It wasn't even proper to whistle, but there was a certain entertainment on summer Sunday evenings when various members of the household took themselves off to the 'preaching'. The preaching was at the schoolhouse down beyond the smithy. It was a much less formal business than going to the kirk, of course. It involved a walk along the honeysuckle hedges and the footpath leading on to the public road, and down the hollow between the drystone walls of fields on either side, here and there catching up with some neighbour also on his or her way to the meeting.

'Who did you see at the preaching?' those who stayed at home would ask. Those who had taken note would say whom they had seen and who was absent, who was sick and who was away visiting a relative. If the neighbour had trouble with straying sheep, or lacked some special thing, that information was imparted to the family. It all provided a pattern to the background of our lives, small talk, a laugh, a sigh of sympathy. Sunday evening closed in on the family like an enveloping blanket, as the shadows crept across the court. The lamp was never lit while a streak of red or orange remained in the sky, the northern lights perhaps, the last glow of a perfect day, a day apart from the other days of the week. The ploughman or the byreman came back from his visit to his relatives, trundling his battered old bicycle into the side of the gighouse, the collie dogs stretched their legs and came to lie down beneath the kitchen table.

A Galloway Childhood

How well I remember my grandmother saying 'Will you say grace, James?' to a dear relative and the endlessness of that blessing.

I used to think of all kinds of things to keep my mind from the food before us; from the apple tart and jug of thick cream, the stacked shortbread, the cherry cake, the floury scones, the sponge sandwich, to say nothing of the ordinary things, the inevitable chickens sitting side by side awaiting demolition. Old so-and-so's grace was a homily on the growth of corn, the temperature of hell and the narrowness of the narrow way to heaven. I much preferred the minister's sense of proportion. After all, his living depended upon making The Word appeal, but old so-and-so could inflict his grace whenever his audience could be caught on one foot, for who could be so un-Godly as to protest?

My Childhood

Visitors put in an appearance at all times of the day. The ballad singer – there were still a few about in that part of the country even then – might show up in the mid-morning.

My Childhood

Callers on bright sunny days had to be content with the company of the women of the household, but in the evening there was time to relax; to stretch one's legs and take a breath of peat reek, listen to a story and tell one in return. On summer nights, tired from a day in the hay field or at corn harvest, grandfather was never too weary to give his 'crack' to a visitor. After supper, so long as the fire glowed, he would talk. On such nights the sunset was slow. The gloaming lingered and the night held off its blanket. How often have I seen it ready to settle round the place, yet holding off; the sun like a burning ship away beyond the horizon, the night as quiet as the flight of a gliding bird, with such peace as is in the flow of the river in the small hours of the morning, and yet not the silence of death, for the mice would be squeaking in the corn thatch and the owlets mewing in the shadows of the trees.

My Childhood

Grandmother and my aunts were friendly with Miss Dunbar. They had a feminine love of very proper tea parties. Once in a while they simply had to get out the finest set of china, the best silver tea service and the biscuit barrel and entertain Miss Dunbar, and I think that although the visits of Miss Dunbar often clashed with more important work, they put themselves out to lay a table for her benefit. She came, on these occasions, reeking of mothballs and paraffin, dressed in her best black dress, her large bonnet and a comb in her wonderful white hair, and was received like the lady she was. I cannot remember those conversations when Miss Dunbar came to tea. My most acute memory is of being uncomfortable because I was on my best behaviour. I remember her visits because I squirmed and suffered strain until she departed, much in the same way as I did when the minister came and his wife played the piano and sang a song.

My Childhood

When I was very small, and the company all many years younger, I remember him rising to dance a reel to the music of the gramophone, and what a dangerous place was the floor of the kitchen for a toddler trying to cross from one side of the room to the other while eight people were spinning and turning. Although he was slightly lame in one leg, for he had broken an ankle as a boy and never had it set correctly, grandfather was light and graceful on his feet when he danced. He liked to watch the dancers too, when he was older and unable to join in himself, and he would sit with his stick between his knees, beating in time with the music upon the tiles at his feet. Clutag house saw many a lively evening when the long nights set in and the gale tugged and pushed at its thick walls, managing to do no more than make a rumbling in the chimneys and a howling sound in the key-holes. A singer was always welcome and the songs they sang are rarely sung now. I think now that I was living at the very end of that age when a family found its entertainment in simple homely ways, entirely unselfconsciously.

My Childhood

It was all a great mystery to me, the beginning of this thing, the way it went on, the completeness of the transformation from peace to bedlam. The evening might be quiet with one reading under the spilled light of the oil lamp and another busy darning a sock and all that could be heard was the steady, melodious ticking of a clock and suddenly the gramophone was out, the table pushed back and everyone was dancing. No one complained it had been a hard day ploughing the old fallow or mowing in the five-acre. No one said anything about milking in the morning or the tasks that still had to be done before the light was turned out and everyone toddled off to bed. Dance, they said. All at once life had to be brightened, the house made to resound with the whirling of feet on tiles, the music of an old, scratched and sorely misused record. Dance, they said. Man wasn't put on earth to do nothing but toil. Sometimes he had to let him-self go and do his best to remember the steps, whether he had once been correctly taught or not, whether he knew the refinement of the ballroom, had worn white gloves and ball-room shoes, or never danced in anything but farm boots all his life. When it was over the house seemed to go abruptly to sleep, the rain spattered on the skylight, the wind moaned in the chimney, the last glow of the embers faded and the cats snored. Sometimes I sat up late and went to bed so stimulated by it all that I couldn't sleep even when I was enfolded in the softness of a chaff mattress.

A Galloway Childhood

The most hopeful time of the day is surely when the day begins, when day comes like a great forest fire taking hold, in a blaze of red and gold shading to a mellow yellowness. Mornings were quiet save for a bird calling somewhere out in the moss or a beast lowing in the pasture. Whoever rose to start the day, to fan the embers of the almost dead fire with a folded newspaper, set the kettle to boil and draw water from the pump, looked to the east and thought the world was wonderful. So it was. It was never more wonderful except perhaps when there was no day of work to be faced and morning grew into noon and we were all enjoying a life of ease, off by the sea. The marvel of the new day might have tarnished a little by the time the family were all hurrying about, when milk-pails were rattling and churns being rolled and horses were led by the forelock down from the dew-drenched field.

'We'll go to the shore on Sunday. What do you think?' Someone would say. 'If Father says the weather will stay.' The sun would break from the sheltering hills to bathe fields of swedes and white and purple-blossomed potato fields in its magic light. Whoever had the inspiration would stand and

stare at the barley and oats, the broad acres of dairy pasture, and admire the silhouetted trees and the endless, snaking dry-stone walls and repeat, 'On Sunday we'll picnic at the shore.'
A Galloway Childhood

On Sunday morning the work went on at a feverish pace. On this depended the time of departure, and departure in itself was an event. The kitchen was a bustle of comings and goings as one came with a bundle of kindling, some paper and a box of matches, and another carefully packed cups and saucers in a great pan basket. The kettle? Had someone carried the kettle away? No use going without a kettle and a teapot, and none of your dainty little china teapots, but the kitchen teapot that held a pint or two. Another scuffle while someone fumbled through to the settle for newspaper in which to wrap both the kettle and teapot, for they were sooty things and Mary or Ellen would be wearing their best dresses and didn't want soot spoiling their appearance, even on the lonely shore at the Black Rocks. Had the travelling rug been put out. And a few oilskins? At the end of the day grandfather might toss these into the trap with an 'I-told-you-so' look, but by then the magic of the day at the shore would have mellowed all.

Departure was a timed thing. Three or four leaving on bicycles, for the folk at Hillhead were joining us, and the rest crowding in the trap, so tightly that without the precaution of a well-fastened door someone might land on the road. One person remained at home, perhaps the most jaded, worn-out member of the family, content to toddle off and spend the afternoon reading a book. Through the march gate, and on to the road, with the pony giving a little toss of his head as he broke into a trot, listening all the while to the chatter of excited boys.

My Childhood

The journey took us across the moor, through fir plantings, up the grey road to the country schoolhouse, which stood in isolation behind a more solidly built dry stone wall than those that divided adjoining fields, and over a rise to the deciduous trees that were commoner than pines and larches in the woods above the shore. The cottagers' dogs barked as we passed and hens scampered in front of the wheels of the gig while the children of the little stone houses stared at us or shyly waved a greeting, but our thoughts were elsewhere. We were eager for the first glimpse of the sea. We could already hear it and smell the sea weed, or so we fancied, when we still had a mile or so to go. The pony quickened his pace as he went down hill. He, too, knew we were near the sea and the end of our journey.

'The sea! The sea!' we cried and there it was, a pale blue haze between the fluttering foliage of the trees, as blue as the soft blue of the sky and almost indistinguishable from it.

A Galloway Childhood

The younger members of the family were excused. They could run helter-skelter for the water's edge, but the elders had work to do. One started off with the kettle and a cup to get water from a well, another moved boulders and constructed a fireplace, while a third freed the pony and tethered him on a long line so that he could graze on the fine grass and move a little through the gorse. The travelling rug was spread and the loaded baskets brought down. A fire was kindled in the new fireplace and the virgin stones blackened as the kettle was set to boil. Perhaps then they would come down to look at the sea and examine our finds among the seaweed, the putrifying seabird's carcase that had an irresistible attraction, the shell of the crab, the piece of the lobster pot. Once I found a notched stick. A cousin, like the rest of the family, fertile in imagination, explained to me that it had belonged to a sea captain who had perished in a wreck. Each notch represented a member of his crew put to death for mutiny. There were at least thirty notches on the stick. What terrible things happened at sea.

We could hardly wait to paddle, and old and young divested themselves of boots or shoes and stockings. Great aunt kilted her dress as far as decency and dignity would allow, an inch or two, and did her feet good, even if the pebbles made her wince. The heat mist would be over the water more often than not and a line of cormorants would appear and disappear again as they flew low along the bay. The tide, fallen back from the rocks, would leave deep pools isolated. The bottom of these pools was smooth rock. Here and there were small boulders and among them lurked crabs. How often we slithered and fell into these pools. The seabirds called. The little rock pigeons flew in and out of the cliffs and the cries of the family went unheeded until the air itself directed us to satisfy a ravening appetite.

My Childhood

I found my first partridge's nest in the Wee Five Acre. I caught an eel in the water that ran under the bog field, shot a pheasant on the Big Hill, fished a trout from the burn in the Wee Field and stalked a hare on Clutag Hill. How many times did the march pool flow over my boot heads! I saw these fields in root and grain and gathered mushrooms from their ancient turf. I walked them in the silence of daybreak and stumbled through them when night obscured the whitewashed walls of home. Somewhere in the peace of early summer I heard the yellowhammer's song. I must have been very young when first I heard it, but the sweetness and the sadness of it impressed themselves upon me so that I am again a child when I hear it now, just as I am at home when I hear the curlew's cry.

Pastures New

The end of many a harvest comes at the start of another and is no more than tail corn and chaff, but although we talk of the cycle of the years, we overlook the fact that we are involved in the cycle ourselves. Time produces a head of corn or an oak tree and the corn and the tree come in time to harvest so that there is perhaps some excuse for reminiscence and nostalgia. My memories are pleasant ones of summers, springs and winters, with the ploughing finished or the sowing done and the peewits were crying over the moss. I travelled back at that time with a heavy heart, knowing that grief was upon us and it was unlikely that a pony and trap would meet me at the station. There was a cruel bite in the last breath of winter lingering in the high hills. Grandfather had died two days before. I came back to a loved and familiar place, walked up the steps and entered the house to breathe again the woodsmoke and hear the clock chiming. There is great comfort in a handshake, in a steady look of understanding.

On the following day the minister came and a great gathering of farmers, farm workers and country people assembled at the steading. I shook hands with old men I had never seen before, men in caps, men in hard hats, bare-headed men; with old friends and old enemies, like the gamekeeper who came to pay his last respects.

It is odd how a generation of men seems to topple like corn. In just over a year both grandfather's brothers followed him to the grave. Farms changed hands and old, treasured things were sold, among them the anvil, the bellows and the ploughs of which he had been so proud.

My Childhood

The moor, or the far moss, as it always was to me, was just another field, a field with a boundary that was the sky, a dead tree, a cairn on a little hill, a mound where the blaeberries grew.
Pastures New

There's nae finer place, boy, than working in the fiels. There's jist you an' the Lord God and the green grass. Nocht metters.
Wigtown Ploughman

. . . a distant prospect of Snowdonia, a glimpse of the Berwyns, the yellow grass of the bleached moorland in winter, brown of peat banks, dark green of heather clumps that changed to purple in August, and the delicate shading of the moss of the Migneint, the bogland.
The Idler's Companion

4

From the Far Moss, the Fiels and Migneint

THE TOWNSMAN NAMES HIS STREETS and avenues, his rookeries of flats, his forests of suburban homes. His mental place is in the buildings he has erected, and perhaps he sees beauty there. He must be happy, because he remains in his acres of brick and mortar most of his life. The countryman names his fields or discovers that his ancestors did it for him. The wood has a name, the path has a name and the hill too gets a name, and often they are descriptive of the land, its shape, its crop, its size.

The names of the home fields were all utility ones, giving indication of their locality. Long ago they probably had Gaelic names, but if they had, the names were forgotten. When my grandfather farmed them they got new ones. The field that held the old stackyard and the elms became the Sow's Field. It was given to the pigs, for its crop was stones, mushrooms in autumn and little yellow lilies when the year was young. The Wee Field was behind the house, a sort of sacred field that was never ploughed. It belonged to the hens and the pony. The Switchback Hill ran back from the Big Hill. On the Switchback a lazy man could lie in the sun and let summer take care of the weeds, for no one could see him there. There was the old road field, the bog field, the Wee Five Acre, Clutag Hill, the hill away from the morning sun, the March Gate Field and the Far Hill, or the Low Planting Hill. They marched such places as the Other Clutag Moss and the Malzie Hill, and looked on the Barlae Hill, that always had a horse grazing its steep slope, and the distant hills of Grouse, where the geese were on the green turf and countless sheep bleated through the spring. When these places were as much in my heart as the air of the high hills was in my blood, I wandered the fields, and though noon was warm and a thousand rooks went over before dusk, my days were mostly morning when the light was on the branches of the pines in the garden and hens were cackling in the cart shed.

Pastures New

The corncrake still called from the fringe of the arable country, from little, hidden-away paddocks where the rising hay was dotted with yellow-flowered weeds and seeding thistles. In such places a man would still wade into his meagre crop of hay with a scythe in his hands and a sharpening stone in his hip pocket. The sound of the stone on the blade while the sun rode the summer sky kept the 'crakes silent, but at evening they called again. Only in such places did they survive.

The Way of a Countryman

The Wee Field may have been in crop before I was born – I cannot remember ever seeing it under the plough – but the rest of the farm was cropped in rotation. Each field was cultivated for three successive years and then reverted to pasture. First it was ploughed to ley, that is, first year in corn, then it was put in roots and finally it was 'sown' out. When a field was ley it was hard to plough. It had been trodden hard by cattle. It was well manured. The sheep had grazed it, the milkers had fed over it a thousand times. It was ready to repay the rest. When it was broken the ploughing was the hardest task of the 'back end'. First the headland scrape was made and the rigs marked. This was done by making a sort of false furrow with an extension from the plough. The rigs were paced or measured with a rig pole and finally the ploughing proper started. When a field had not been broken for several years the first ploughing with a horse team is hard on both horses and man. A man who has ploughed a field before knows the boulders and the stoney places, but a man who is fresh to the acre goes warily.

Pastures New

There is a timelessness about ploughing, and there is something in the nature of a field that shows the way of men long dead. The headlands and the drains tell the story of cultivation and a man ploughing looks at the same marks his predecessors used, eyes the same stones in the dry-stone wall, the same boulders in the land, the same ancient hills. He sees the same autumn and spring skies, and the call of the plover and the curlew are as timeless as the air and broken earth.

Country Matters

A field of barley is a richer sight to look upon than a field of oats, though it lacks the beauty of wheat because there is something full and wholesome about the golden wheat dotted with those red poppies that somehow always manage to get sown in a wheat field. The barley is combed by the wind. It has less resistance to the wind than the stronger wheat. It goes down much easier and becomes what is known as straw-broken. Farmers will tell you that strong barley is nearly always short in the straw. The man who cultivates barley with a good head and long, strong straw will make his fortune. Barley lies in places where oats still manage to rise. Almost everyone who grows the crop looks anxiously at his field when there has been a late winter gale. The havoc of a wind needs to be seen to be believed. The slope of a barley field can look like the tousled head of a boy newly risen from bed – except that it can never be straightened again. The knives of the binder will crop the heads and they will tumble to the ground, the combine will drag the straw by its roots and men will have to take time to clear the great harvesting machine of clods of grass soil and tangled straw. A good malting barley is a precious crop. Distillers and brewers buy the grain before it has sprouted but he is a lucky man who cuts a whole field without losing a bushel or two, even in a summer when the sun shines and the corn is cut with little loss of time.

A Fowler's World

All at once, when the harvest fields began to have that brown look that comes as the stubble ages, the goldfinches would be gone. This desertion of a place in which they had fed for several weeks was significant to anyone who watched the changing face of the countryside. Even the burn seemed to have a more sullen flow.

The hawthorn leaves reddened and crumbled. The black-berries, soggy and wormed, fell into the water and stained it, while out in the field the spear thistles changed into bare stalks and the docks rusted.

Country Matters

He stood in the warm evening air after supper and listened to a dog barking far away in some small farm behind a hill. He could see a thin streak of smoke curling above the hill and the quiet evening carried the sound of children's voices as they played in the field in the distance. Everything was so still that he could even catch the drowsy cooing of the pigeons in the woods and imagine the sleepy farms in the red mist of the west where the sun was setting.

Wigtown Ploughman: a Part of his Life

The grass was high, the ditches full of meadowsweet, the water peat marches scented with myrtle.

The Idler's Companion

The trees of the planting had been rooted too close together, so that the spruce died as it grew and lived only at its tip. Most of the wood was of spruce, but here and there a pine towered above its neighbours and a sycamore struggled for life. The strongest memory of that planting, where I had so many adventures, is of the hoarse, endless cooing of pigeons on drowsy sunset summer evenings. The place had an irresistible attraction for me. It had all deep silence and blue shadow mystery that a lonely wood has for a small boy. In its deep shadows there was a sort of heart-pounding sanctity that lasted between the cooing of the pigeons or the startling chatter of the magpies. It fascinated me, invited, whispered and beckoned as the breeze stirred its fern and bracken undergrowth, and when I was no higher than the bracken I responded, treading softly, nervously, through the pine needles, staring at the pencil score marks of fir branches across the sky above my head.

My Childhood

The moor farms were places where black-faced sheep and bullocks were kept and little else thrived save the moor birds, rabbits and adders. The farms were walled in by drystone, grey-lichened walls that ran away back, it seemed to me, to the far end of the world, crawling up long rocky slopes and disappearing into hidden hollows of round rushes, bog cotton, meadowsweet, stands of reeds with waterholes where fowl swam.

A Galloway Childhood

It is strange how the place where man has made his home holds something after he has ceased to live there. I have noticed this thing about derelict country cottages, abandoned farmsteads in the Welsh hills, and there are hundreds of them. At the quarry there was no sign that there had ever been a farm on the spot, or, as grandfather insisted, a bit of a village, a clachan, as we call it in the north. High up on the hill there stood the gable of a cottage, part of a dike now, but down at the quarry I searched for the foundations of the cottages of the clachan. They had been ploughed out, carried away to stone heaps or buried in the bog as it slowly came up the hollow.

Pastures New

It was crossed by a moorland road that hardly ever saw more than one or two vehicles a day and those were horse-drawn carts or gigs. Rabbits, a large proportion of them black ones, bobbed about the road from one side to the other. The road belonged to the wild creatures and not to man at all. Walking along the soft springy grass beside the wheel tracks one could put up a grouse or encounter a fierce falcon perched on a silver birch. The road ran away in to the far distance, straight and true, two stony tracks where the wheels ran, two strips of green and a central stony strip where the hooves of horses prevented the grass spreading. One could have camped on that road, sat down in the middle of the track, or stretched out and gone to sleep there without fear of being disturbed from morning until night – unless a tinker's cart came rolling along to make a short-cut from one of the little villages beyond the skyline to another far out of sight on the other side of the spruce woods.

The Way of a Countryman

Here in the hollow, in the next field, the cattle will shelter. Walk down from the moss in the gloom of lowering night and you will find them along the hedge. The rain that sweeps over the hill sings among the hawthorn branches and steams on the backs of the black and white cows, but they are sheltered here, sharing the corner with a disconsolate horse that remembers the comfort of his stable, the warmth of a straw bed and the infrequent squeak of the rat hurrying across the rafters.

The stubble is bare, but the wind has left a mark on this field. The lying corn could not be lifted far enough to allow the binder or the reaper to crop it short and the straw rots on the field where the short sheaves were gathered. Behind each dike that cuts across the wind the grass is thick and coarse, behind each little brow, and in the lee side of every shoulder, the soil is deeper, for the wind is old. It has blown the earth from a hundred little hills, changed the course of streams that have changed the course of rivers that have made seas.

Pastures New

The water-meadow, in case you are unfamiliar with it, is one of the older devices of those who have cultivated riverside land since man first began to farm. There are, however, thousands of acres of water-meadow that bear no more important crop these days than hay and supplementary grazing for cattle; beds of sedge encroach upon the meadows, and bushes and stunted trees take over, slowing the draining of the fields, creating a place in which the river floods and eddies until it carpets the higher ground with dead grass, rushes, straw, twigs and branches. Some of the older water-meadows have lost their title for they have become a bog in which mace and tall reeds grow. Red-stemmed marsh plants spread their seeds, rattling like pepper pots, showering anyone who passes with a hail of hard seed which falls into the water and never grows but lies there to feed whatever creatures live in the jungle, duck and waterhen, coot, vole and mice. The very nature of such places make them forbidding when the river rises and gently eases hay ricks from their resting-places or backs a barrier of flotsam into the mouth of a drain, stopping the flow, making the ditches far back in the arable land overflow at the cattle drinking-holes. The duck of the river haunt the water-meadows. There is no better place to find them than in the secret corners of the alders away down where the drains have to be crossed warily on treacherously slippery planks or poles covered with a scraping of earth to provide a foothold.

A Fowler's World

I used to walk a snipe bog where sometimes snipe were as thick on the ground as feeding starlings. It was an electrifying experience to visit the bog on certain days. Snipe were everywhere, along the fringes of great pools of clear water in which several feet of sphagnum were submerged, among the rushes and along the narrow tracks on hard ground where the sheep had negotiated their way from one island of fine grass to the next. The rising snipe would begin like the lifting of leaves in the wind. Before one had walked ten yards on a bright morning the snipe would be off to some secondary roosting ground, for they lived on the bog by day and took themselves off at night.

The Way of a Countryman

The Kildarroch burn was a deceptive bit of water. In summer it flowed smoothly under the thorns and brambles and combed the tresses of green grass it lifted from the bank. In the shaded tunnels of the over-hanging bushes, broom and sallow, little moorhens would learn navigation swimming upstream to catch up with their mother. In spring it was different. The water was higher, the thorns were bare or just beginning to bud. Little bits of moss and other debris from flooded banks higher up spun in eddies along with limp, often washed feathers of fowl. The burn had an ominous appearance in the hard bright light of the early months while peewits were calling. A boy who fell into such a burn could be swept away into its cold depths, clutching helplessly at strands of bracken and dead sticks and ending up far down water, 'over his head' and drowned. The family had a love of graphic descriptions of this kind. I drowned several times over just looking at that burn as we jogged past it in the gig, but nevertheless, it had a strong attraction for me. I saw more than my elders saw. I saw the green and yellow trout that lived in the shelter of submerged stones, behind a sunken moss block, a tree fallen from the bank or beneath that floating mane of grass held by a vibrating twig dipping into the current.

The Idler's Companion

There was nothing in the open countryside to indicate that there was a loch out there, but across my path were the winds of a burn that could in winter have been a sizeable river. I crossed it, walking on the boulders and small stones. A shallow stream of water was all I encountered with the exception of a pool or two which I walked round to find a shallow which I could cross without danger of getting my feet wet. The sun shone down on me. A buzzard sailed on the moorland. I saw a merlin. Apart from this I saw no other sign of life, although I could hear the occasional bleat of a black-faced sheep and the song of some small moorbird perching in a thorn. Out there, I told myself again and again, was the loch. It lay in a depression. Its surface was rippled by the breeze, even though I had a feeling it might be more often still and as smooth as glass that mirrored clouds drifting high overhead. Such a dream is the kind of thing that an idler has while he lies back in his chair. It can be quickly dispersed by the reality of a high drystone wall to be climbed or the effort of scrambling up a peat bank and facing the same obstacles over and over again! Dreams are gentler than reality, easier on the muscles, less fatiguing because they exercise only the mind! I went on and on. Even the four ounce Hardy rod became heavier as I carried it. A cleg or two got up from the rushes in a hollow and began to drink my blood. I cried inwardly and hoped that I would soon be rewarded for my pains.

It was as though I had experienced a mirage when I finally crossed a plateau of heather. There in the sunlight was my loch with the golden shore! The burn wound on away to my right. I wasn't sure that it really had anything to do with the loch, but there was no mistaking the place. The fine gravel of the shore was golden. I walked towards it over the uneven peat and through the roots of old heather. I kept my eyes fixed on the water to make sure I didn't miss so much as the smallest dimple of a trout just nudging his nose in the surface film of the water. There was no dimple and no ripple. I should have known there wouldn't be. I had fished a great many lakes and lochs, in all kinds of conditions. At noon on a hot, mid-summer day with no ripple and no sign of a fly on the still surface the loch was dead. There seemed no chance of a fish showing. There wouldn't be until nightfall when the air had cooled. Perhaps then a little breeze would run down the loch, riffling the surface, pushing a fly along, drowning a moth and making it struggle. Then, as they had at daybreak, trout would come swirling up out of the cool depths and gulp down whatever took their fancy. I had come too late or too early, but it didn't matter all that much, I had arrived. I had travelled hopefully. This was the way living should be!

The Idler's Companion

No carrion flew over the mountain, the raven had gone too and the shadows of the valley deepened as the mountains gathered that blue haze that belongs ultimately to the night.

Trout from the Hills

Cefn Garw in the migneint (the rough back place in the bogland is a fair translation of the Welsh) was named for the nature of the place. Everything in Wales is descriptively named, a stranger will discover. The swift is not simply a swift but the 'blackbird of the church'. The sand martin is 'the swallow of the pools' and the buzzard's name – boncath – is said to be derived from Boda Cath, the cat hawk, named for its mewing cry. The rough back place knows the buzzard yet, though Roberts is gone from the farm now. If the old Welshman who named Cefn Garw had thought more about the place he might have used a perhaps more apt description involving the word heddwch, which means peace, for this is the very atmosphere of that bowl of the moor where the greystone buildings dominate the scene. The eye alights on the steading almost instantly because there are no other buildings there. Such fences as there are out there blend into the background of the marshland.

The Idler's Companion

The huddle of stone buildings perched high on the slope above the river was constantly attacked by the weather. The high wind's fingers felt under slates to see if they could be lifted from the nail-sick rafter and sometimes succeeded, stripping first one and then another

The Idler's Companion

The spring had lost itself in the grass. The last of the scrawny fowl had been chewed up by the fox. Occasionally a ruminating ewe took shelter from the hot sun and left her droppings on the doorstep, or a hank of her shaggy fleece on the fence. Who would exist there but a ghost? When I go again to fish the flats of the river at the bottom of the marsh I know he will be up there, watching me, and taking note of all the other small, insignificant things that happen in the course of a day. I know him well now, and understand what it was he loved most about the place, its depth of silence, its being outside time and the chiming of a clock, the awesome quality of such a vast landscape with no one in it.

The Idler's Companion

Set in the Machars of Wigtownshire, Scotland, and particularly in the locality of Malzie School, the Malzie farms and the district bounded by Wigtown, Kirkcowan, Mochrum, Portwilliam and Sorbie, this is the story of part of the life of a ploughman, son of a cotman. Cotfolk are the dwellers in the small stone cottages which house the agricultural workers of the north. Part of the life of a simple man of the soil, this story refers to no particular ploughman, for all are not great fighters, poachers, drunkards or wife-beaters. This story is an attempt to portray something of the best and the worst in them.

Only those who live near the soil can see true beauty; few can know beauty when it is before their eyes. I make no ambitious attempt to give a conception of hidden beauty, but offer a humble story of the things that the eyes of thousands have seen in the country, and, I fear, their minds have forgotten.

The text will clarify the dialect, which has been written phonetically as far as possible. Geographical detail is more or less preserved, although, for the sake of the story, farm names and names of characters have been invented to suit what is purely fiction. No reference is made or intended to any living person. As for the harshness of this tale … there is no need to invent truth. Would you have me tell you a fairy story?

5
First Words
Wigtown Ploughman: Part of His Life

CORMORANTS STAND ON THE ROCKS of the Port William shore of Luce Bay. Long-necked, ungainly black birds, they stand there while the incoming tide creeps up the shore and mist drifts across the bay and up the glen to the Alticry lodge. When the rocks are awash, the birds rise and fly slowly, less than three feet from the surface, out over the water, where they vanish into the mist. The gulls remain afloat on the swell and great waves crash with thunder on the shore. The crash echoes up the cliffs and fades into a soft sigh.

When the cormorants come back through the swirl of the mist they are flying higher. Their arrow formation mounts into the rain; wings beating fast, then pausing in a glide. They rise above the shore and the heather slopes that run down to the sea, pass over the fir and spruce wood that shelters the Alticry road as it falls to the beach, and fly on over green hills and white-washed cottages nestling beside stacks of peat.

This stretch of Wigtownshire, the Machars, sticks out like a spearhead into the sea and is bounded by Luce Bay on one side and Wigtown Bay on the other. Cormorants fly often across from the Bay of Wigtown to the Luce Bay, crossing rough moorland, smooth red-earthed country dotted with quiet farms and small plantations, artificial coverts for the pheasants. Like black geese, the cormorants seem, only that they make no sound, flying unheeding of the life of man below.

Running eastward from Alticry, the hard grey road winds by a lattice-windowed lodge, a stone cothouse, a lonely school, and four or five farmsteads, before it reaches High Malzie. There is a signpost at High Malzie pointing the way to Whauphill in the south. Ahead lies Wigtown, but first the road throws off a branch to Kirkcowan on the left, and afterwards passes a cluster of houses named Hillhead, standing up off the roadside on the right. Farther on is Barness farm overlooking the Bladnoch, which winds away northward to Kirkcowan. Bounded by stone dykes, the road rises and dips till it drops suddenly to run beside the Bladnoch to the straggling village of Bladnoch itself, where the water streams under a bridge to meander between muddy banks to the sea.

Back along the road, past Hillhead and round the bends to the High Malzie signpost; retracing these steps up the road toward Alticry, can be seen, now on the right hand, the ruins of a cothouse, just past the dwelling of a herd, where the mossland stretches into the distance like the soft brown skin of a deer. Only the walls at either end of the ruin are standing; a monument to the lives of cotmen a hundred, perhaps two hundred, years ago. The stones where once there was a fireplace are blackened with the smoke and heat of fires that fell in dusty embers on bygone winter evenings. The broken remains of slates and glass strew the floor, and weeds grow between the stones of the crumbling walls. The place is desolate and scarce a soul passes it in the course of half a day. The mossland to the north is a barren expanse of peat holes and heather banks, while in the south its tail-end meets the sweep of the hills and woods.

It was in this ruin, on the edge of loneliness and time eternal, that Andy Walker lived with his wife Sarah in 1907, but it was no ruin then. The walls were white, the slates intact, the windows cracked but whole. The shaws of potatoes littered the garden; hens scraped in the furrows, and a lean, half-starved collie slept on a stone flag at the door when it was dry. The garden was fenced with strands of barbed wire, to which clung tufts of sheep's wool; the rails of an old iron bedstead, an ill-built dyke, and three thorntrees.

It was not strange that Andy, a ploughman, should live back there where only shepherd folk or herds lived. He worked at the farm of Drumlin, a hilly place off the Alticry road some three miles from his cothouse. In November 1907 he brought his wife there after their marriage. She had already borne him two sons out of wedlock. One was a strong boy of five and the other was three. It caused little stir that Andy should marry Sarah, for many men did not marry until their intended wives had demonstrated their fertility, intentionally or carelessly, once, twice or even three or four times.

Sarah was pregnant in the summer of 1907, and in November another son came. With no ironical intent the first legitimate child was blessed with his father's name. They named him Andy Walker. The other two were James and William, although to their father they were Wee Jimmie and Wee Wullie.

Andy Walker, ploughman, was short and thick-set, with black hair. His rugged face was always adorned with a black stubble. Yet the stubble, by virtue of a weekly shaving with a none too sharp razor, never developed into the promised beard. Andy was a good man, a grand worker, not too often drunk, but hard on his wife. Sarah at twenty-five was a great fat wench. She had borne eight children. One had died and five in all had been fathered by Andy. Her lawful husband, as was the custom, forgave her previous follies and stipulated only that the results of her former adventures in love did not eat the food which he worked for or share the roof he provided for her. And was this ungainly baggage his first folly? – there were stories bandied among the gossips of the coutryside of three or four women who had mothered his seed; of five children in all that he had sired when the down of youth was still on his chin.

Born in a cothouse near Stranraer, Andy had served many masters before coming down to the Machars. He had since ploughed for the McDowals, Kellys, Pattersons, Littles and Craigs. At twenty-eight, when his indiscretions loomed larger in his mind than ever before, he took Sarah Todd, the redoubtable servant of a farmer near Newton Stewart, to be his wife. The marriage was celebrated in the style of the cotfolk, with drinking, brawling, arguing, singing, coarse joking and uncouth laughter in the cothouse that the two made their first and only home. Twelve men, eight women, and three or four children crowded the small dwelling.

Some were sick, all, even the pale-faced children, were drunk. There was laughter and ribaldry until the early hours of the morning, and Andy was not sure for a week or two whether his wife had slept her first night with him or one of his bosom cronies. Yet even that, had he been sure of the offence, would scarcely have disturbed him. For better or worse they had taken each other and for better or worse would they remain together. At least that was his feeling when they were first married.

The child Andy was born when the ploughing was at a standstill. At birth he was a yelling red lump of flesh that tore and struggled at his mother's breast like the overgrown calf at the teat of the cow. No doctor attended the event. Instead a 'freen' from the Port sat with Sarah in the dim light of the November afternoon while she laboured. Andy cut the shaws and lifted turnips on the hill above Drumlin, for the plough was at the smithy. Sullen in face of the visitor's knowing looks when he came in at night, he sat down to untie his sweaty boots with only a word of enquiry as to whether the thing was a girl or a boy.

With his father asleep on the floor, his two brothers rest-lessly lying by his side, Andy the younger first saw the light on a Sunday morning when the rain lashed the windows and the wind howled round the four walls of the cothouse. The room stank with the odour of unwashed bodies, a dirty collie, dungy boots and damp clothes. It was a wet, cold Sunday when no dinner, scant meal at best, was served; when the door was only opened as his father went to relieve himself, or empty a handleless pot that served the sick woman as a commode.

Half the day had passed when Andy drew his damp tweed trousers over his hairy buttocks and tucked the tails of his grey flannel shirt between his legs. At once roused out of the stupor of its sleep, the collie rose and slipped out as Andy opened the door to heave the contents of the pot over the potato patch. It returned again with its hair matted with rain and mud when he went for the third time to perform the same duty. It was into this atmos-phere that Andy, the baby, was born.

Nothing untoward in the type of household in which he first breathed the humid air of life. From the Isle of Whithorn to Glenluce, from Loch Ryan to Glen Trool and Creetown, throughout the length and breadth of the Lowlands and Highlands of his rugged native country, the same cothouses stand as the birthplace of thousands of humble folk of the soil. The same squalor, the same one-roomed dwellings with cracked tile, or rough earth floors, untidy fireplaces, torn clothes, creaking bedsteads, faded willow-pattern crockery, smoked ceilings of wood, and the same pungent smell of baby napkins.

It is strange how the poor folk of the earth, living on the meanest of life's requirements, seem to thrive and reproduce, coming up again in the next generation stronger than ever before.

His mother, untidy, slovenly, bedraggled creature, was in keeping with her household; one of hundreds of cotwomen. Creatures of toil, cow-like solidarity, placid, unthinking females mated to hairy, wiry men who work under the open sky and ask nothing of life but to be allowed to live. Their toil is wearisome and endless. A battle waged year by year with the wind and the rain. A fight for a good harvest, hoeing in the chill days of spring and working in the broiling heat of midsummer, turning hay and forking sheaves.

None, except the romantic who revels in the work of Robert Burns, would expect the son of such people to be unusually brilliant. The opened eyes of the newly born Andy held no sparkle of promised genius. His head was small, even for a baby; the thin legs kicked feebly from the red flesh that was his body, and the surest indication that the creature was born of higher intelligence than a calf was the ferocity with which its hands clawed at the breast of its mother. Sarah had lost interest in it; it was the result of so much pain and discomfort, nothing more.

It had to be fed, and when it cried she gave it her breast. No such thing as chivalry prompted the father to sleep on the floor for a night or two. Chivalry was far above the finest aspects of his character. The coldness of the floor was preferable to the bed which smelt strangely like the byre at calving time. The groans of his wife from time to time, and her restless shifting about on the torn sheets, would have made sleep impossible.

Unable to lie still on the floor any longer, he rose just before dusk and struggled into his jacket. Half a day lying on his back was irksome to a man whose normal days were spent cleaning stables, wheeling great barrow-loads of dung, ploughing, harrowing and trudging along sodden furrows with his boots weighed down with clinging soil so that they could not have been heavier if they had been lead.

The strong smell of his pipe drifted across the room as he slid his feet into his boots. He did not trouble to tie them but tucked the laces into them and clattered over to the door. The peats in the fire blazed suddenly as the draught rushed in and dust rose from the embers to float in white flecks over the bed. His wife, as she reached down for the milk jug by the bedside, heard him spit even above the roar of the wind. He coughed and cleared his throat with a hollow grunt that might well have been the cough of a sick cow in the byre.

The two boys wailed with hunger, but their mother was too fatigued even to call to them. They prowled round the room and dragged a half-empty jam-pot from the table. It slipped and fell with a crash that made the baby start. They sat down beside the broken pieces, dabbling in the jam with their grubby hands and sucking their fingers. When all was quiet once more, the woman in the bed fell asleep. Her sons finished the jam. The hairs of the dog, picked from the floor with the gooseberry pulp, were sucked down their hungry throats. Then Wee Wullie discovered a hole in a sack of potatoes that stood in the corner. These they gnawed with quantities of the black earth from the bogland in which they had been grown.

There were many such dreary days in November, for it was a cold and wet month. A few days after the birth of Andy, Sarah was on her feet again; not that the cothouse was cleaned, but the fire was brighter; the dog turned out in the morning; the strong smell of life was dispelled when the freezing blasts of wind were admitted as she opened the door. The ancient clock on the wall ticked again after she had balanced somewhat unsteadily on a chair to wind it; life went on as before. Her husband came home in the dark with horses' hairs clinging to his coat and the smell of their sweat on his hands. He would light his pipe and doze in the firelight with his socks steaming on his feet. The three children were asleep when he returned each night, bringing with him the rain from the fields. It trickled from his leggings and topcoat and formed a pool behind the door where he hung his outer clothes on a nail. His dark face glowed with the cold and his ears stood out red from the sides of his tweed cap.

At the end of the month the weather changed. The swamped land froze solid; the north wind chapped the naked face and hands, and the turnips in the field snapped off when men tried to pull them. Only in the sheltered fields were they able to plough. Andy ploughed under a clear sky. Not a mist or rain came with the wind for weeks. The puddles at the stable door were solid like white marble. On the icy roads horses slipped and skinned their knees, and many a high-stepping trotter that had been the envy of the countryside had to be shot where it fell on the brow of glassy hills. It was the hardest frost in years. Milk in cans froze overnight and there was no water to be had.

Wee Andy was unaware of it all. He lay snug beside his mother's warm body, crying when he was hungry, and wetting the sheets when fed, so that his legs became fired and sore for want of attention.

It was poachers' weather. There were fine moonlight nights when a man could see almost as clearly as in daylight, and the shadows by the fir woods were deep and friendly to those who wandered abroad hunting for game. Andy prowled with his dog and gun in search of rabbits, hares, roosting pheasants, or even a cock from an unlocked fowl-house. Shooting by such bright frosty moonlight was simple, and when the iron pot bubbled at night the tempting flavour of a mixed stew mingled with the other odours of the cot-house. Snare wires hung in a bunch behind the door and a dozen wooden pegs dried in the oven. In a box covered with wire netting were two red-eyed ferrets. Wee Wullie, who was particularly interested in them, was bitten badly for his pains and brought the house down with his screams for an hour afterwards.

Once poaching gets into the blood of the countryman he cannot resist the lure of frosty nights when the moon shines. When he can walk over hard-frozen furrows; steal along the shadow of a hawthorn hedge between one and two in the morning and lay the long nets, whistle the dogs softly, and lift the squirming bundles of furry life from the meshes. With the moon on the windows of his lonely cothouse he lies unsleeping on his bed. He watches the stray clouds that flit across the lime whiteness of the moon. He sits up and gazes longingly across the hoary fields and imagines the bag that awaits him in the quietness of his favourite glen.

Then, if his blood is thick and has a trace of the adventur-ous spirit of his wild forefathers in it, he will rise, pull on his clothes in the chill shadows of his bedroom, put a string through the collar of his dog, and roll his nets. No one sees him as he opens the door, which through the day creaks and grates along the tiles, yet in the 'wee sma' 'oors' opens with magical silence. His heart beats fast; his hands tremble and his boots clatter for a moment on the stones by the door. Maybe the hens in the nearby shed scold him for disturbing them, with that strange crooning sound that is half a whistle; or a fence will squeal its protest as he straddles it; maybe the iron shod on his heel roots a stone from the grass; but he hurries off in to the ghostly moon-light with the night air reviving a sleepy body.

There were nights when Andy lay in his bed but little, when he crawled up ditches and stole along the lonely dyke-sides. The misty beams followed his dark outline through the marches of Malzie, over the hills of Clutag and into the shadows of Barnbarroch woods. The beams found him in the quiet fields of Sheep Park or by the burn at Capenoch, his collie tripping daintily by his side, the nets hidden by the roadside or amongst the whins, and a heavy bag across his back carrying thirty or forty rabbits to the shed behind the cothouse. Four pheasants roosting close together on the low branch of a fir tree, or a curious hare standing in silhouette on rising ground were marks for his shots.

Who heard the roar of the gun in the wildness of the mosslands, or who cared if their slumber might have been disturbed by the crash of a stone falling from a dyke near at hand? No one heard the excited yelp of the collie as the rabbits ran blindly into the stretch of net, or the whack of the experienced hand as it broke their necks.

A nine-mile cycle ride to Newtown with seed bags full of coupled rabbits was a profitable journey at four o'clock in the morning. Often the bodies were still warm as the bike sped into the sleeping town to a house where the dim light burned and the goods were delivered and purchased. A brief greeting; the emptying of the bags; price quoted; reduced, and accepted; another brief farewell after a pause to light a pipe, and the bike would speed away down the road again. A note or two crinkled in the pocket. There was the exhilaration, the profit, the adventure and the thrill of it all, to urge him to do it again another night.

Andy's days were tiresome, half asleep in the stable at dinner-time, wearily jolting along the furrows behind the plough in the afternoon. In the evening home to bed till the moon rose and then up again and away across the quiet hollows, through drowsing farmsteads bathing in the light of the clear night sky.

Bibliography

Wigtown Ploughman: Part of his Life (Putnam, 1939)
The Poacher's Handbook (Heinemann, 1950)
Fresh Woods (Heinemann, 1951)
Pastures New (Heinemann, 1952)
Trout from the Hills (Heinemann, 1961)
The Way of a Countryman (Heinemann, 1965)
A Galloway Childhood (Heinemann, 1967)
A Fowler's World (Heinemann, 1968)
The Idler's Companion (Heinemann, 1978))
Feathered Friends (Chatto, 1984)
Country Matters (Gollancz, 1984)
Ian Niall's Complete Angler (Heinemann, 1986)
My Childhood (Clutag, 2004)

Little Toller published a compendium edition of *Fresh Woods* and *Pastures New* in 2012 and Birlinn released a new paperback edition of *Wigtown Ploughman: Part of His Life* in the same year.

Acknowledgements

My thanks to my family and friends for encouraging and supporting me in the putting together of this anthology and to Robert for everything.